Gods and Myths of the Aztecs

Gods and Myths of the Aztecs

Norman Bancroft Hunt

SMITHMARK

This edition first published in 1996 by
SMITHMARK Publishers Inc., a division of U.S. Media Holdings, Inc.,
16 East 32nd Street, New York, NY 10016

SMITHMARK books are available for bulk purchase for sales promotion and premium use. For details write or call the manager of special sales. SMITHMARK Publishers, 16 East 32nd Street, New York NY 10016; (212) 532 6600.

Produced by Regency House Publishing Limited,
The Grange, Grange Yard, London SE1 3AG

ISBN 0 7651 9901 7

10 9 8 7 6 5 4 3 2 1

Page 2: The Two Lord, Ometecuhtli, who was both male and female and the supreme creative deity in the Aztec pantheon. This seated figure shows him in the form of Tonacatecuhtli, the Lord of Fate.

Page 3: Relief showing the Feathered Serpent, major symbol of Quetzalcoatl, descending between two symbols of years.

Above: Maya culture, The Temple of the Sun and its courtyard in Palenque, circa 600 AD.

Right: Xolotl, sinister twin of Quetzalcoatl, was the planet Venus as Evening Star.

Jacket front cover: Mask representing Chalchihuitlicue, 'Lady Precious Green', who was a fertility goddess and consort to Tlaloc, the Rain God. Insets top: Erotic figures from the Colima/Nayarit border, 300 BC-100 AD. Centre: Pottery ocarina in the form of a turtle. Aztec. Below: Coatlicue, the Earth Mother, one of a pair of colossal statues which stood in the courtyard of the Great Temple at Tenochtitlan. Back cover: Pottery figurine of the Lord of the Dead, Mictlantecuhtli. On their way to his Underworld, the dead were reduced to skeletons by a Wind of Knives. Totonac.

CONTENTS

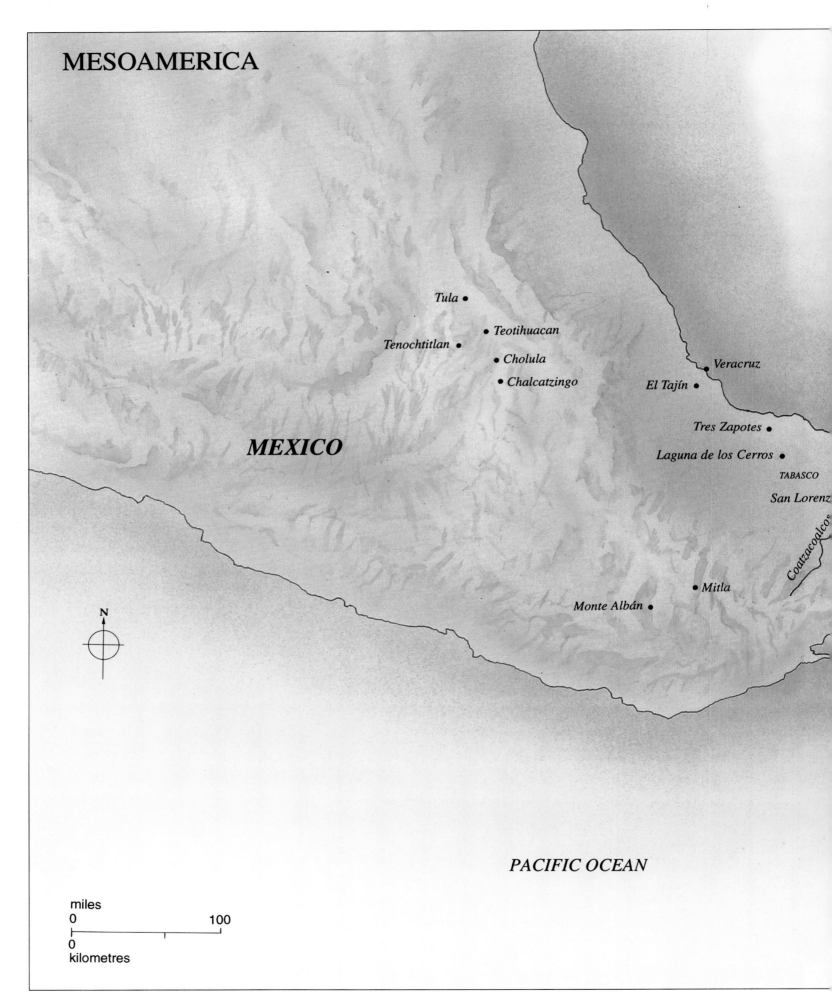

MESOAMERICA

Tula •

• Teotihuacan

Tenochtitlan •

• Cholula

• Chalcatzingo

Veracruz •

El Tajín •

MEXICO

Tres Zapotes •

Laguna de los Cerros •

TABASCO

San Lorenz

Coatzacoalco

• Mitla

Monte Albán •

N

PACIFIC OCEAN

miles

0   100

0

kilometres

Gulf of Mexico

Isla Cozumel

• Chichén Itzá

• Mayapan

Jaina •   • Uxmal

Caribbean Sea

YUCATÁN PENINSULA

• Villahermosa

Calakmul •

BELIZE

• La Venta

El Mirador •

Palenque •

Uaxactún •

Tikal •

Piedras Negras

• Lubaantun

PETÉN-YUCATÁN
LOWLANDS

• Chiapas

Bonampak •

Altar de Sacrificios

• Caracol

Gulf of Honduras

CHIAPAS

GUATEMALA

• Playa de los Muertos

Quiriguá •

• Copán

• Izapa

HONDURAS

• Kaminalujú

EL SALVADOR

7

INTRODUCTION

The Old World of Europe and the New Worlds of the Americas were unknown to each other prior to 1492, when Christopher Columbus sailed across the western ocean in search of a route to the Indies. Although Columbus did not realize he had discovered a hitherto unknown continent, by the early 1500s a permanent Spanish presence had already been established in Hispaniola (Haiti and the Dominican Republic) and in Cuba. The expeditions of Hernandez de Córdoba in 1517 and of Juan de Grijalva in 1518 to the Yucatán Peninsula and to Tabasco in Mexico returned to the West Indies after bartering glass beads for objects made from gold, and this stimulated the governor of Cuba, Diego Velásquez, to outfit a formidable expedition to exploit the wealth of the new lands they had discovered and to claim them in the name of the Spanish crown.

Thus, in early 1519, Velásquez appointed the 30-year-old Hernan Cortés as his commander to investigate the lands occupied by people whom the Spanish knew only by the tribal names Culhua and Mexica. The tentative explorations of Córdoba and Grijalva had already been noted by an indigenous leader known as Moctezuma, whose emissaries had met Grijalva and reported back about these white men with beards who had arrived from across the seas in strange ships. He also knew of their aggressive intentions, since the Spanish had displayed an evangelical zeal to dominate the nations with whom they came into contact. Moctezuma must have considered Cortés' arrival with some trepidation, since

he had reports of the Spanish fomenting trouble and encouraging dissent among a number of tribal groups who were subject to Moctezuma's own rule. Moctezuma's tribute collectors among these peoples had been mishandled by the Spanish and it was clear that a confrontation with the Spanish was imminent.

Cortés did not, however, realize that the might of imperial Spain was to be tested against that of another great empire: the Aztecs. Nor could he have realized the long traditions that had culminated in Aztec dominance of Mexico, and which had resulted in Moctezuma ascending the Aztec imperial throne in their capital city of Tenochtitlan (present-day Mexico City). Also unknown to Cortés was that the Aztecs had built a civilization which was in many respects comparable with the highest achievements of the Old World in Mesopotamia and Egypt: including the erection of massive temple pyramids, the development of an hierarchy based on inherited privileges, and the establishment of extensive trade. They came from backgrounds dominated by royal lineages and in which the acquisition of power and wealth were important; and they were both religious zealots: Cortés with a tradition that dated back to his studies of Roman law and his conviction that he was destined to establish Spanish sovereignty and Spanish belief in the new lands he came to conquer: Moctezuma with a belief in his own incarnation as the Sun deity of the Aztecs with an inviolable right to rule by reason of his descent from the royal families of the Aztec ancestors.

Although Moctezuma had only consolidated his

This mosaic pectoral ornament was worn by an Aztec priest of Tlaloc, the Rain God, and symbolizes the lightning snake as the precursor of thunderstorms.

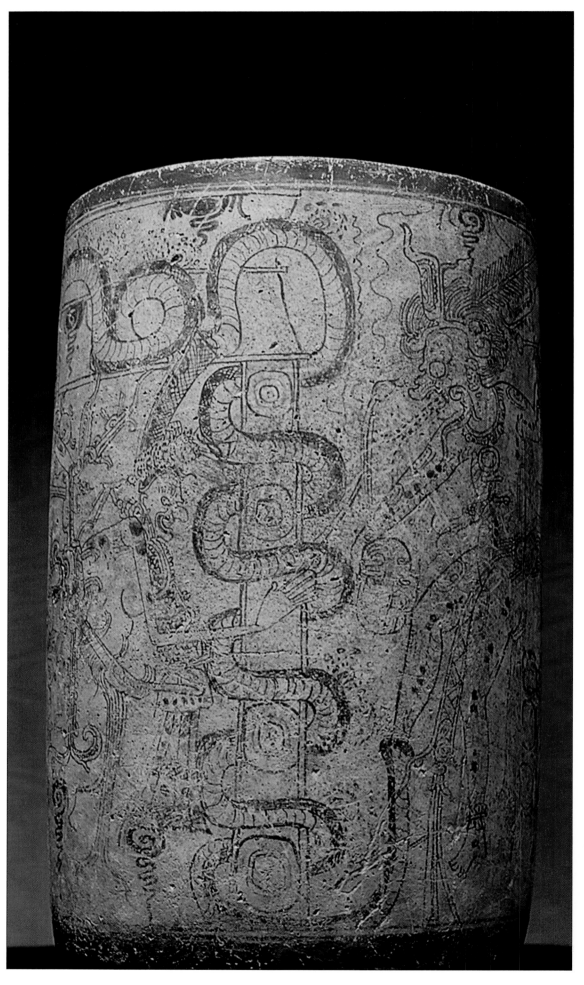

The serpent as a creator deity was important throughout the Mesoamerican area and was associated with powers of underwater and rebirth. Maya.

power in 1508, just 11 years before the arrival of Cortés, the traditions he inherited can be traced back over 3,000 years. This book introduces the traditions, beliefs, and attitudes that governed the Aztec world-view and which were to appear so strange to the Spanish invaders of the New World. To understand this, we need to consider how the Aztec world was created and the beliefs that underlie Aztec thinking,

the roots of which can be traced back in the origin myth of another culture: that of the Maya.

In the beginning there was only sky and water and the world was in darkness. Coiled in the water lay the Feathered Serpent, Gucumatz (Quetzalcoatl), surrounded by a glittering array of sky-blue feathers from the raxom bird and green feathers from the tail of the quetzal bird. Above, in the sky, dwelt Heart of

Heaven appearing as three kinds of *huracan*, or lightning. At first all was silent, but then Feathered Serpent and Heart of Heaven began to speak to one another, and from their words and thoughts alone the mountains and earth rose from beneath the waters and the animals were created. Feathered Serpent and Heart of Heaven told the animals to praise them in their prayers, but the animals were only able to utter cries and growls. They were devoid of speech and unable to praise the gods by naming them.

Since the animals were unable to praise them, Feathered Serpent and Heart of Heaven told them to retreat into the forests where they would be hunted and sacrificed in the offerings that the people to come would make in the gods' honour. Thus they decided to make people who would have the power of speech, and they fashioned a man out of clay. But, although the person they created could talk, the words it used made no sense and its body was weak and crumbled to dust. When the rains came and the rivers rose the clay man dissolved into nothing. Heart of Heaven and Feathered Serpent then consulted the aged diviners Xpiyacoc and Xmucane, the Grandmother of the Day and the Grandmother of the Dawn, who used maize grain and red seeds from the *tzité* plant to count the days of the sacred calendar.

Xpiyacoc and Xmucane decided that men should be made from wood and women from rushes, and as soon as Feathered Serpent and Heart of Heaven spoke and thought these words the world was populated. But these were wooden people, without hearts and without emotion, with no blood in their veins and cold, expressionless faces. So the gods made a great flood during which resin fell like rain, and then they sent fierce demons to destroy the people and told all the animals and the people's utensils to rise up and crush their faces. The leaders of the demons were *xecotcovach*, the eagle; *camazotz*, the vampire bat, which cut off the heads of the wooden men and who lived in the east; *cotzbalam*, the jaguar, who lay in wait for his prey; and *tucumbalam*, the crocodile of the west. The wooden people attempted to flee, but most were killed. Those that escaped fled into the trees where they became the forest monkeys.

Still lacking the prayers of the people to sustain them, the gods decided to send the Twin Heroes to destroy the monsters of Xibalba, the Uderworld, and to obtain maize, the flesh of the people. From maize the people were created. The maize people possessed great wisdom and clear sight, and were able to see through the earth and sky to the limits of the universe. Soon the chief of the maize people, Vucub-

Caquix, or Seven Macaws, became vain and arrogant. He likened himself to the Sun, though Sun had not yet risen, and claimed that his beauty surpassed that of the Moon, though Moon had yet to be brought into being. This troubled Feathered Serpent and Heart of Heaven, for the people were too much like themselves and controlled power that only the gods should control. To diminish this power Feathered Serpent and Heart of Heaven breathed on the people and, like mist forming on a mirror, the powers of the maize people were dimmed. Finally the people separated, going in different directions and speaking different languages, then, when the Morning Star rose, the gods and the most powerful animals were turned into images of stone. It was in this manner, according to the Popol Vuh, the Sacred Book of the Quiché Maya, that the world was created and populated.

Our knowledge of the Popol Vuh is thanks to an obscure seventeenth-century Spanish priest, Father Francisco Ximínez, whose parish was in the village of Santo Tomás Chichicastenango in the highlands of Guatemala. The sixteenth-century original is lost, but Father Ximínez made a copy (in Latin characters) from the original manuscript which he had borrowed for this purpose from one of his Indian parishioners. The Popol Vuh presents an account of the Quiché Maya world: their cosmology, mythology, traditions, and history. Prior to the Spanish conquest of New Spain (central and southern Mexico, Guatemala, and northern Honduras and El Salvador) in the early sixteenth century, the Quiché Maya had developed a powerful culture in the Guatemalan highlands, containing elements that we now know to have been widespread throughout the area known as Mesoamerica. Thus the Popol Vuh illustrates a number of characteristics of Mesoamerican cultures: the twin aspects of sky and earth, the fearful nature of the gods and animals, the use of calendars and writing, the power of the spoken word, the symbiotic relation between man and maize, and the monumental carvings in stone that were erected at ceremonial centres.

Mesoamerica is, however, an enigma, since it is neither a single culture area nor an homogenous geographical region. The term has been coined by the anthropologist, Paul Kirchoff, to identify that part of Mexico and Central America which the Spanish considered to be 'civilized' when they arrived during the 1500s. Kirchoff has defined this as being represented by at least some of the following culture elements: monumental architecture in the form of temples and pyramids, widespread human sacrifice, a sacred calendar on which ritual activities were based, hiero-

glyphic writing, ritual ball games, a pantheon of olds, *chinampa* (or raised-field) agriculture, marketplaces, and a well-established trading network. Such definitions are useful in academic enquiry, since they enable research to be carried out within clearly defined parameters, but they tell us little about the people who lived in this area. The researches of the archeologists and anthropologists do, nevertheless, provide us with some insights into what the lives of these people may have been like. Archaeologists, who work with the remains of past civilizations, uncover artefacts from which we can deduce certain usages and thus make educated guesses about the ways in which the people lived. Anthropologists, whose main concern is with historic cultures, give us some ideas as to how ancestral links have been maintained, and we can use these to reinterpret the evidence from the past.

In Mesoamerica this past is a long one, since it stretches back to the Olmec cultures of the tropical lowlands of southern Veracruz and Tabasco of about 1500 BC, although their antedecents had already formed small villages associated with rain and fertility cults as early as 6500 BC. The Olmec elaborated on this pattern by introducing more intensive agriculture, based on the staple foods of maize, beans, and squash, and this enabled them to support larger settled communities in localized areas, which, in turn, led to the development of a ritual complex based on ceremonial centres that were the focus of religious life for the nearby villages. Excavations at the principal Olmec sites of San Lorenzo and La Venta reveal a fascinating world of human-animal gods presided over by a ruling élite of priests and shamans. Although the early Olmec period is still shrouded in mystery, it is becoming increasingly clear that their influence was widespread throughout Mexico from about 1500 BC until the sudden, and unexplained, demise of their culture about 500 BC.

Olmec influence is apparent in the symbols used by the Zapotec of highland Oaxaca, from whom we have the first calendrical systems and use of a written language from about 600 BC. Here, too, we find evidence for astronomical observations in the alignments of ceremonial buildings, tombs containing rich grave goods and suggestive of a 'royal' lineage, together with indications of elaborate public ceremonies presided over by the priests. The Zapotec were a fiercely independent group who, although they traded with their neighbours, nevertheless maintained their capital city of Monte Albán as a free state until the arrival of the Spanish.

West of the Olmec and also showing indications

OPPOSITE
Sacrifices were often made in order to appease the deities. This stone carving (Palma) was part of the ritual regalia associated with public ceremonies, and shows a prisoner with hands bound behind his back. Totonac.

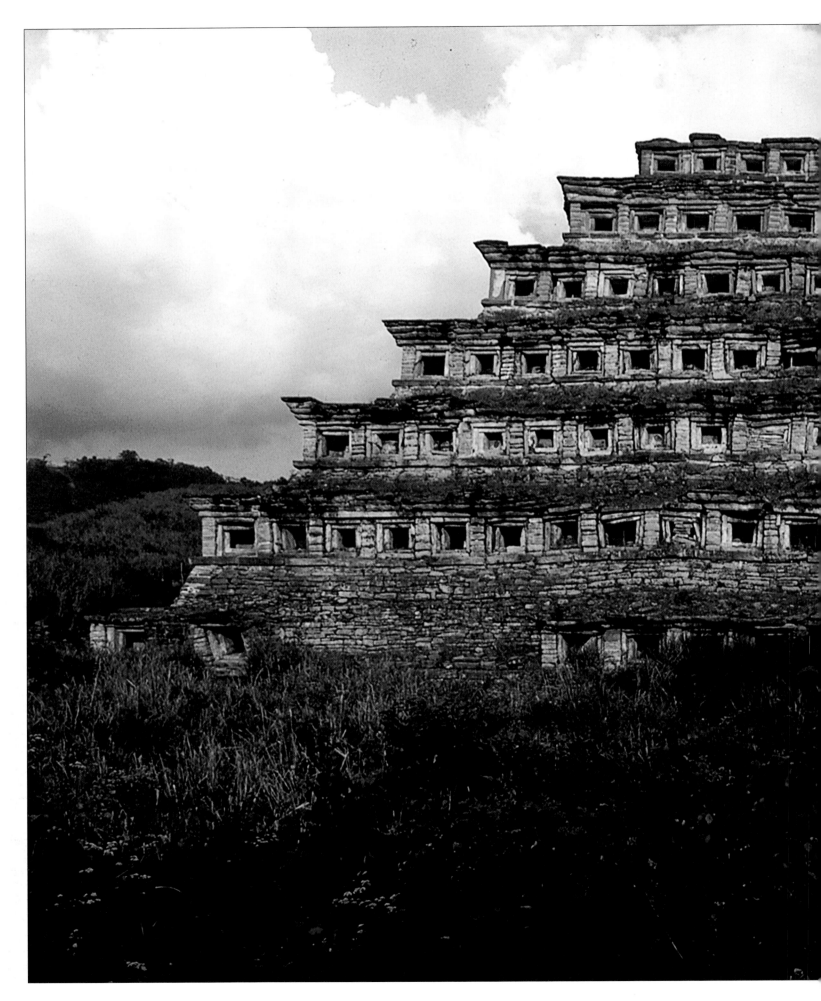

The Pyramid of the Niches at El Tajin near Veracruz. The façade of the building is formed from 365 niches covering all four sides of the building and is representative of the days of the year. Each niche originally contained a statue of the patron deity of each day. Totonac.

of their influence were the Maya, in the Yucatán Peninsula of Mexico, Guatemala, and the adjacent regions of Honduras and El Salvador. Early Maya culture began about 300 BC in the Petén area of south-central Mesoamerica, with major ceremonial centres at Uaxactún, Yaxchilán, El Mirador, and Tikal. Mayan power and influence grew rapidly, and soon Tikal, as well as other major complexes with elaborate pyramids supporting temples, became the focus of ritual observations for very large urban populations. The ceremonial centres in many instances became virtual city-states, each ruled over by a dynastic family and an élite priesthood. Other major centres, which were to continue to flourish until about 900 AD, are at Palenque, Uxmal, Copán, and Quiriguá. During this period the first evidence of human sacrifice and blood-letting as a means of propitiating the gods becomes apparent.

Parallel to the rise of the independent Maya centres, since there was never any Mayan national state and the different centres were often in competition with one another, a true empire was being built in Mexico which centred on the imperial capital of Teotihuacan, and which had other outlying cities of

RIGHT
This stela depicts Quetzalcoatl wearing a characteristic headdress, necklace and earrings. The star-shaped carving on his chest represents the wind jewel symbolic both of the wind and compass points. Totonac.

FAR RIGHT
Stone stela carved with symbols of a sacrificial heart and earth monster. The monster appears in the form of the Serpent associated with Totonac earth deities.

OPPOSITE
This shell-encrusted helmet from the Toltec capital of Tula depicts Quetzalcoatl rising from the jaws of the earth, which is here represented in the earth deity's form of the Coyote.

major significance such as Cholula, Xochicalco, and El Tajin. At the height of Teotihuacan power, the imperial city had a permanent population in excess of 200,000 and was characterized by massive pyramids, palaces, and market places, with monumental sculptures dedicated to the gods of rain and war. The cult of the Jaguar, first developed among the Olmecs, is apparent here, as is that of Feathered Serpent who, as we have already seen, was an important deity among the Mayans. Like that of the Olmecs, Teotihuacan influence was widespread and maintained by an elaborate system of trade routes that embraced virtually the entire Mesoamerican

Mosaic plaque showing Quetzalcoatl rising from the earth in his form as the Morning Star. Such plaques were used to record astronomical events and it is likely the image used here depicts a passage of Venus, since this planet was associated with the Morning Star.

area. Teotihuacan appears to have been diffusionist rather than expansionist, since there is little evidence to suggest they made any attempt to subjugate neighbouring tribes. Their influence stemmed from indirect contacts and trade, and it is clear from the archeological record that certain sectors within Teotihuacan itself were occupied by 'ethnic' minorities and specialist artisans from other regions. For unknown reasons, Teotihuacan suddenly collapsed about 700 AD. The imperial city was razed by fire, many of the monuments were mutilated, and the

great palaces were reduced to rubble.

Mythology tells us the destruction of Teotihuacan was the result of argument between the noble families who claimed allegiance to the deity Tezcatlipoca, or Smoking Mirror, and Topiltzin Quetzalcoatl, Our Young Prince the Feathered Serpent, who left Teotihuacan as a result of disagreement about the succession to the rulership. After many wanderings, he is said to have founded the city of Tula, the Place of Reeds, where he was established as priest-ruler. Whatever the truth of the myth and what its relation to the fall of Teotihuacan may be can only be conjecture; however, there can be no doubt from the archeological record that the cult of the Feathered Serpent flourished at Tula under Topiltzin Quetzalcoatl's patronage and that of his descendants. For 200 years, from 900 AD to 1100 AD, the people of Tula and its outlying centres, known to us collectively as Toltec culture, became the dominant force in the area and extended influence over other neighbouring groups. Thus, for example, the Mayan city of Chichén Itzá in the Yucatán Peninsula shows two clearly defined building phases: an early, and purely Mayan, complex of buildings known as Old Chichén, and a newer complex built by Mayan labour but under the direct influence of the Toltecs which includes numerous carvings that clearly reflect Toltec ideology and belief.

The power of all the major centres appears to have waned by 1100 AD, perhaps as the result of warfare among dissenting subject groups, or possibly due to the expansion of population which meant that local villages and farms were no longer able to support the large numbers of people attracted to the urban communities. It is also possible that epidemic diseases played an important role in the depopulation of the ceremonial centres. Although the people did not disappear, indeed the Mayans are still the majority in the modern Mesoamerican countries, many of the ceremonial centres were abandoned and the populations dispersed. Other changes, however, were taking place. By about 1200 AD small groups of mercenary warriors, the Chichimeca, migrated into the central plateau where they assimilated many of the cults and beliefs of the Mayans and Toltecs. Gradually they consolidated their power and founded the city of Tenochtitlan (modern Mexico City) on a number of swampy islets in the Lake of Mexico. Another Chichimeca group settled the nearby island of Tlatelolco. By 1425 AD Chichimeca power in the region was undisputed. Tenochtitlan then formed an alliance with Tlacopan and Texcoco in an effort to subjugate their neighbours, including Tlatelolco, over whom Tenochtitlan imposed its rule. The allied groups called themselves the Triple Alliance, but they are more commonly referred to in the literature as the Aztecs. Under the Aztecs, Mesoamerica was subject to a terrifying rule by force. Formidable Aztec garrisons were stationed at subject towns and the greatly feared tax collectors demanded excessive tributes that had to be paid annually to the ruling

This lithograph by Frederick Catherwood gives an indication of the ruined state of Mayan ceremonial centres when they were first explored during the 19th century. The stone carving in the foreground showing the Feathered Serpent would formerly have been placed in the plaza where rituals took place. Pyramid of El Castillo.

élite at Tenochtitlan.

Under the Aztecs, and unlike the independent city-states of the Mayans, ultimate power resided in a single individual: a living representative of the creative forces that brought the Aztecs into being. The hybridization of Aztec culture is apparent in the fact that such a priest-king could only come from a family who claimed descent from the Toltecs, the descendants of Quetzalcoatl, the Feathered Serpent. The guiding deity of Aztec culture was not however Feathered Serpent but Tezcatlipoca, the Smoking Mirror, patron of war. Although the Feathered Serpent was important to the Aztecs – in fact, the priests who conducted human sacrifices were known as Quetzalcoatls – it is apparent that Feathered Serpent and Smoking Mirror were in opposition to each other. One was the god of creation, who, under the instigation of Topiltzin Quetzalcoatl, was propitiated by offerings of flowers; Smoking Mirror, however, was propitiated by the offering of sacrificial human hearts. The irony in Aztec culture is that the god of flowers, Feathered Serpent, officiated over the offerings of human hearts to his rival, Smoking Mirror.

The final phase of Mesoamerican culture began in 1503 when Moctezuma Xocoyotzin came to the throne. As a direct descendant of the Toltec kings, Moctezuma claimed the authority of Feathered Serpent, but he also had a presentiment that Feathered Serpent would return to Tenochtitlan from Tula to overthrow his rival, Smoking Mirror. It was said in the ancient myths that the representatives of Feathered Serpent would appear as strange white men with unfamiliar clothing who would walk across the water to destroy the power of Smoking Mirror and that this would coincide with Ce Acatl (one reed), the end of the Aztec 52-year calendrical cycle. The end of each 52-year period was, therefore, marked by elaborate ceremonies and sacrifices to appease the gods and to ensure that the cycle would be renewed, and was consequently a period of uncertainty and tension.

By a coincidence of fate this cycle was due to be completed in 1519, and during this year Moctezuma started to hear rumours of white men who had arrived from across the seas. These referred to the expedition of Hernando Cortés, who had sailed from Cuba with the hope of finding unimaginable wealth in Mesoamerica. Moctezuma, however, must have seen his arrival as an omen of the confrontation between Feathered Serpent and Smoking Mirror. When the Spanish *conquistadores* defeated the Aztecs they were bringing about an outcome that had already been predicted in Aztec myth.

Feathered shield bearing a mosaic that symbolizes a whirlpool, which was one of the manifestations of Chalchiuhtlicue whose name translates as Lady Precious Green and who was an important goddess of fertility among the Aztecs.

CHAPTER ONE
THE OLMECS: ORIGINS OF AZTEC CULTURE

The Mexican scholar, Miguel Covarrubias, refers to the Olmec as the 'Mother Culture' of all later Mesoamerican developments, and until recently it was thought that all of these could be traced back to the Olmec groups living in the lowland regions of southern Veracruz and western Tabasco near the Coatzacoalcos river on the Gulf of Mexico. We now know, however, that the Olmecs were actually several independent groups that were part of an increasing urbanization of Mesoamerica which was brought about by the development of maize agriculture. That the great ceremonial centres of the coastal Olmecs should have impressed themselves on archeologists is due, essentially, to their size and to the fact that they are located in areas where investigation has been possible. Olmec remains in the heartland of Mesoamerica are only poorly understood due to the dense vegetation. We therefore rely for our knowledge of Olmec culture on the principal sites located on or near the Gulf coast, although it is apparent that numerous other sites have yet to be discovered or investigated. This Gulf coast area is eminently suited to large scale agricultural practice, since the region permits maize growing year round and seasonal flooding has built up a deep layer of fertile soil along the river levees. These are the most productive lands in all of Mexico, and it was this that enabled coastal Olmec culture to flourish and prosper.

The favourable conditions in the area meant that the large settlements in this region were the most influential of the various communities that began to be formed some 3,000 years ago, and Olmec 'style' art and architecture is apparent in regions far removed from the river levees. Recent investigations, in fact, indicate that the Olmec area is one of the most important archaeological zones in the world, with a density of sites that is unparalleled elsewhere in the Americas, and it is apparent that the major centres were the focus of ritual activity for urban populations numbering several thousands. Although working with 'mute texts' – stones, architecture, carvings, pottery, and other non-perishable remains – must always leave important questions unanswered, the archaeological sites are, with more intensive investigation, beginning to tell us a great deal about the lives of these ancient peoples.

Olmec influence appears to have been due to a diffusion of ideas rather than conquest, since there is no evidence to suggest that the Olmecs were particularly warlike or expansionist. It may even have been the case that expatriate communities of Olmecs occupied parts of other city complexes in the Mexican highlands, since recent work at Tlatilco, on the north-western edge of Mexico City, and at Chalcatzingo, located about 75 miles (120 km) south-east of Mexico City, has revealed considerable sub-floor burials and bas relief carvings that are unmistakably Olmec in origin. One of the carvings at Chalcatzingo, for instance, depicts a seated woman ruler wearing a skirt and a fabulous towering headdress. She is seated on a throne inside a cave-like opening formed by the characteristic gaping mouth of the Olmec Serpent deity. Another carving

nearby depicts two warriors holding a captive, and they are shown wearing Were-Jaguar masks that are synonymous with Olmec culture.

Although the Olmecs were not the peace-loving ambassadors and diplomats they are sometimes depicted as being, for we have evidence in the form of carvings which definitely show Olmec warriors, their captives, and the destructive attributes of some of their gods, it would appear that they generally maintained relatively cordial relationships with their neighbours and were more interested in trade contacts than conquests.

In fact, they seem to have been mostly concerned with the aggressive and dangerous forces that were thought to permeate their own world than they were with any threats from outside communities. Carvings depicting the forces of the sacred sky, earth, and underworld are abundant at Olmec ceremonial centres, and among these are fantastic representations of dangerous and violent human-animal deities such as the Human-Jaguar, Jaguar-Bird, Bird-Jaguar-Alligator, and Human-Alligator, as well as representations of other gods such as Rattlesnake, Harpy Eagle, Shark, and Monkey. Such deities indicate the Olmec concern for creatures of the tropical forest and seacoast. Other forces of the earth are represented too, as in the great earth pyramid at La Venta which represents a volcano. This close relationship with the immediate environment and the forces it contained is also apparent in the Olmec use of natural forms as places of special significance. Caves, hills, and cliff faces are all demarcated as sacred spaces through the use of carvings and paintings.

It is nevetherless clear that although the Olmecs were concerned primarily with the local environment and the forces they felt were expressed within it, they initiated – or, at least, had the most powerful expression of – a deeply felt link between humans and nature. This, undoubtedly, was an inheritance from the earlier hunter-gatherers who were dependent on game animals, fish, and the seasonal ripening of fruits and berries for their survival. We find among Olmec carvings many indications that they were reliant on the intercession of shamans – people with special powers which could influence nature – as must have been their precursors in the region. The Olmecs, however, began to incorporate these forces within their art and architecture, and thus introduced a form of symbolism and iconography that was to become characteristic of all the later Mesoamerican cultures.

Highly typical of this symbolism was the manner in which space and time were organized as dual

Thr Rain God, Tlaloc, was traditionally believed to live on the tops of mountains where he gathered the rain clouds together to act as his messengers as a sign that he was pleased with sacrifices and devotions made in his honour.

and mutually dependent aspects of sacred belief, and it is only through an understanding of this that we can begin to appreciate the complex cosmologies of later expressions such as those of the Aztecs. It is, however, only recently that these aspects of Olmec thought have become clear. Until the chance discovery in 1965 of a greenstone carving of a figure at Las Limas, Veracruz, it was thought the Olmec religion was a monotheistic one, based on a Were-Jaguar deity which was represented as a human infant with jaguar features. This particular carving was inscribed with representations of other Olmec deities, which had previously been thought of as totemic symbols of the ruling élite. It is now known

that the Olmec world was one in which a host of different powers played a major part, and in which the great ceremonial centres were organized not only as places of pilgrimage and devotion but as representations of myths and beliefs. Thus the organization of a sacred precint became expressive of the way in which space and time were believed to interact to create an environment imbued with supernatural power.

This use of space and time is particularly evident at the great Olmec centre on the island of La Venta, in Tabasco. At its heart is a cluster of mounds, carvings, and temples which are aligned with astronomical observations and arranged in such a manner that the relationships between the buildings

reflect calendrical notations. Thus the architectural plan of the site, including the pyramid at its centre representing the sacred volcano, is expressive of mythological episodes. When the shaman-priests conducted rituals by leading a procession from one part of the complex to another they must, in essence, have been re-enacting a journey made previously by one of the deities and recorded in the mythology of the people. In addition, the relationship of one building to another and its reflection of calendrical notation means that the buildings must also have been expressive of the particular time of year at which such a ritual was destined to take place.

It is, unfortunately, impossible for us to know exactly what ritual performances took place at La

Venta. It is too far removed in time, since La Venta was occupied between 900 BC and 400 BC, and the destruction of the site makes further archaeological investigation both difficult and inconclusive. Many of the monuments have been removed to a public park in Villahermosa, Tabasco, to protect them and it is no longer possible to study them *in situ*. What we do know, however, is that the architects of La Venta and other Olmec ceremonial centres planned the buildings and the distribution of monuments in accordance with a ritual calendar based on careful and accurate observation of the movements of the sun, moon, and stars, and which was interpreted in terms of episodic periods recorded in myths. Far from being a simple monotheistic religion based on

LEFT
A relief carving showing a warrior dressed in traditional costume and carrying a shield decorated with a spiral pattern. As a symbol of longevity, the spiral helped ensure that the warrior received the gods' patronage during battle. Olmec.

the worship of an animal deity, as had long been thought, Olmec culture is now emerging as a highly sophisticated civilization which was at least equal to Old World developments in Egypt and Mesopotamia.

The relationship between humans and nature is further expressed at La Venta by the discovery of buried offerings. Among these are huge mosaic pavements depicting a Jaguar mask which are laid on clay that had been imported from many miles away. Why the Olmecs made such an effort to import clay and to lay out minute stones to depict the Jaguar which was then immediately buried several feet deep is a mystery to us, but the connection between the Jaguar and the Earth is clear. Also discovered at this site was a group of jade and serpentine figurines arranged so as to depict a ceremony. They were buried and marked, so they could be recovered later. Each of these figures is exquisite, and they are supported by narrow upright celts which may represent the basalt columns erected in the monuments above ground. Whatever other significance such offerings may have had for the Olmecs, the fact that they were deliberately interred is of paramount importance and indicates a belief in the presence of powerful underworld spirits that were directly involved in human affairs.

A belief in underworld spirits also helps to explain the meaning of a number of Olmec architectural features that have long puzzled specialists of Mesoamerican cultures. For want of a better term, these have generally been labelled as 'altars' although there is now universal agreement that they never functioned in this capacity. Such altars are found at La Venta and elsewhere and are in the form of rectangular blocks of stone, on one side of which is a recess from which a priest-ruler or a man-god is seen emerging. These figures are frequently combined with Jaguar or Serpent motifs. Given the Olmec belief in an underworld and the importance of caves as sacred sites, it is likely, therefore, that the altars are actually depictions of the emergence of the priest-ruler or man-god from the Underworld. We can also surmise from the fact the figures in these carvings have attributes of both the human and the sacred worlds that the Olmec priest-rulers were not thought of simply as representations of the deities but were more closely associated with the gods as their personification on earth. We might therefore reinterpret these architectural features as representative of the emergence of the original Jaguar God from the Underworld, so that his power could be expressed in the human realm via the priest-ruler

ABOVE
Small figurine of a woman wearing a shell pendant. Such pendants were used as indicators of status by important members of Olmec communities. La Venta.

OPPOSITE
The head of the man shown here bears markings on his cheek which may represent either face painting or tattooing. The head is carved in the form of a hacha *which was worn as part of ritual costume during ceremonies related to the ball game. Olmec.*

33

who, thereby, became the incarnation of the deity itself.

The meaning of the altars does not, however, end with a statement about the link between the upper and lower worlds and the status of the priest-ruler. On many of these carvings the Jaguar man-god emerges from between the jaws of the Serpent, which frame the recess, and he is shown holding a rope which passes around the block and is tied to a captive or slave carved on the surface of the stone opposite

to that on which the man-god appears. From the mythology of the Aztecs, we know the Serpent was a symbol not only of the underworld but also of fertility and procreative power, and that this was closely associated with rivers, springs, and *cenotes* (natural wells). Thus the man-god, or Jaguar, not only emerges from the Underworld but is actually born from the Serpent. In other words, the Serpent gives birth to the forces that permeate the Olmec world. In this respect the Quiché Maya statement from the Popol Vuh, quoted in the introduction, that in the beginning all was darkness and below, in the waters, lay Feathered Serpent who, with Heart of Heaven, brought the world into being through his words and thoughts seems to relate to a very ancient tradition that originates among the Olmecs. In addition, the power of the man-god is further expressed by his capture of a 'slave', indicating that Olmec beliefs – most probably by diffusion, but possibly by conquest – were being incorporated among the traditions of

ABOVE
Bas relief carving of a jaguar which forms part of a decorative frieze on the northern side of the Pyramid of Quetzalcoatl at the Toltec capital Tula.

OPPOSITE
A ceremonial jade adze bearing characteristic Olmec markings. Of particular note is the cleft forehead which is a feature of many Olmec carvings of this type.

neighbouring groups. Also significant is the fact that many of the Olmec carvings depict the Were-Jaguar as a human-animal infant; that is, as the new-born offspring of the Serpent deity which is expressed in the human world as the Jaguar God.

This nature-human relation is also found in an Olmec bas relief from Chalcatzingo, where the priest-ruler or man-god is depicted as sitting in a cave holding a box surrounded by clouds, water, jade, vegetation, and a stone that represents the earth. We must see in this a combination of all the forces that were controlled by Feathered Serpent and Heart of Heaven, as well as the emergence from the underworld represented by the Jaguar God. There is a combination here of powers that reside in the sky, represented by life-giving rain; of fertility and growth, shown by vegetation; and of the powers of the Underworld, represented by stone. Our 'mute texts' are gradually revealing a great deal about Olmec ideals, and these help to explain later developments that reached their final expression in Aztec culture. Although it is a painstaking process to extract information from archeological sites and from little understood carvings and architectural arrangements, it is becoming increasingly obvious that the Olmec world-view was never a simplistic one.

One further aspect of Olmec culture needs to be considered. This is the discovery of six colossal stone heads found at the Olmec site of La Venta, which was fully formed by 1200 BC, and of similar, though smaller, heads found at San Lorenzo. The La Venta heads, up to 9ft (2.8m) in height and weighing as much as forty tons (40642kg), along with a number of other huge monuments, are carved from stone that had been transported from the Tuxtla Mountains, nearly 45 miles (72km) away. Each of the heads is clearly intended to be a portrait of a specific individual, and this has given rise to speculation that they represent priest-rulers and served as a record of the genealogy of a 'royal' lineage. That they must have had a ritual function as well is evident from the fact the giant heads were found lined up along the edge of a ceremonial area.

Even more important, perhaps, are the deductions we can make about the Olmec's way of life from the discovery of such massive monuments. We can guess, for example, that Olmec society was organized in terms of a social hierarchy with a dominant ruler at each of the ceremonial centres, rather than forming an empire or unified state such as was to be typical of the later Aztecs. We can also surmise that these centres were occupied by high status individuals with responsibility for maintaining the ritual cal-

Tlauixcalpantecuhtli, in his guise as the planet Venus, passed through both beneficent and malevolent phases during part of the Venus cycle. He is shown here in a detail from the Cotex Coapi attacking Ocelot warriors. The spear thrown by the god has passed through the warrior's heart. The markings on the left are date glyphs indicating the specific Venus cycle to which the drawing relates.

endar and ensuring that ceremonies were carried out. Certainly the centres – in spite of their size – could not have housed a labour force large enough to have transported and carved the massive stone monuments, and it is therefore likely that the majority of the population lived in outlying hamlets close to the maize fields and only came to the centres on auspicious occasions or to attend particular rites.

Such considerations as above enable us to understand that Olmec culture must have been very highly organized and that political and ritual leadership was invested in a relatively small group of high status individuals. These individuals, as we know from the carvings, were associated with the human-animal deities that were thought to populate the Olmec world. Many details of fabulous costumes marked with name signs, or glyphs, are found at the centres, and from these we can now begin to understand the complex relationships which existed between people and the gods as well as the kind of social stratification that marked Olmec society. We also know, from the evidence of widespread Olmec influences as well as the presence of precious celts and figurines in jade and serpentine, that trade played an important part in the lives of wealthy and high status families. Furthermore, the concentration of such wealth goods at the ceremonial centres confirms the impression given by other evidence that these centres were home to the leading members of the community rather than to a 'peasant' class of manual workers.

But Olmec culture is not without its mystery. For an unknown reason, the great centre at San Lorenzo was destroyed in about 900 BC. All the monuments that were above ground were desecrated by slashing, grinding, slotting, pitting, and so forth, and were then dragged out of the centre and lined up on the nearby ridges. After this they were all buried and San Lorenzo was abandoned. A similar paroxysm of destruction was enacted at La Venta in about 400 BC, and in almost identical fashion. Once again all the above ground monuments, including the massive stone heads, were mutilated and defaced. This, in fact, marked the apparent end of Olmec civilization. The populations dispersed and the reign of the richly clad priest-rulers seems to have been broken.

Just what it was that caused the destruction and abandonment of the Olmec sites will probably never be known. Various theories, including revolution, invasion, or ritual destruction have all been forwarded as possible causes, but the Olmec left us no record other than the mutilated ruins of their ceremonial centres. Only one site, at Tres Zapotes, seems to have carried on any tradition of the old high civilization, and forms a link between the Olmecs and the later Mayans. The most significant find at Tres Zapotes is of tremendous significance in the development of Mesoamerican cultures. Known to us simply as Stela C, it is a carved stone post depicting the familiar Jaguar mask on one side. On the reverse, however, is a deceptively simple arrangement of bars and dots. From studies of Mayan carvings we know that these bars and dots are actually date glyphs, indicating that the late Olmec had already begun to develop the calendrical and written systems that were to be so important during the Mayan and Aztec periods that were to follow.

The Monkey God, Ozomatli, was an important figure in Aztec and Maya mythology. He is shown here in his guise as the patron deity of writing. As the servant of Xochipilli, the Monkey God also acted as a messenger between deities and the people.

CHAPTER TWO
THE OLMEC INHERITANCE

Following the collapse of Olmec culture in about 400 BC, most of Mesoamerica, and particularly the Valley of Mexico, reverted to an earlier pattern of small hamlets linked to low temple platforms. Whatever characterized the Olmecs had become so subsumed or transformed that it was barely recognizable, and due to the propensity of later groups to rebuild over earlier sites there is little known for much of the area from this period until approximately the beginning of the Christian era. What is clear is that Olmec culture virtually disappeared after the destruction of sites such as La Venta.

Elements of Olmec beliefs, although in a much changed form, are nevertheless found among the Zapotec of the Valley of Oaxaca and their linguistic relatives, the Mixtec, in the Oaxaca mountains. Both the Zapotecs and the Mixtecs, unlike many other Mesoamerican groups, retained their independence until finally overthrown by the Aztecs in the late fifteenth century. The early period of Mixtec culture is virtually unknown, but it is assumed they lived in small scattered mountain villages. Olmec influence on the Zapotec, however, is much clearer, stemming mainly from intensive archeological investigation at their hill-top site of Monte Albán. Monte Albán was founded in about 500 BC and continued as a powerful military, cultural, and political centre until it began to decline after 800 AD, partly as a result of conflict with the Mixtecs.

At Monte Albán we find evidence for the further development of a number of traits that are deemed to be characteristic of Mesoamerican cultures; in par-

ticular, the complex arrangements of temple mounds and plazas, an increasing use of a ritual ball game which has its roots deep in Olmec culture, elaboration of writing and the calendrical system, and numerous carvings depicting rulers and deities. Many of the carvings show scenes of ritual bloodletting. One of the temple platforms at Monte Albán, for instance, is faced with stone slabs bearing bas relief carvings of nude male figures with closed eyes, open mouths, and often with mutilated genitals from which blood spurts forth in flowery patterns. This form of sacrifice is well known from later periods as a form of penance practised by celibate priest-rulers, so it is apparent that much of the later belief of Mesoamerica was already being practised by the Zapotec.

Also apparent in the carvings are glyphs which have been deciphered as indicating the names of rulers slain as sacrificial victims during wars of conquest, or those of towns conquered by the Zapotec and paying tribute to the rulers of Monte Albán. Thus between 500 BC and 200 AD the Zapotec consolidated their control of the Valley of Oaxaca, creating a truly urban state ruled over by a divine priest-kingship. The close link that was felt to exist between the people and their environment among the Olmecs is also recognizable in Zapotec architecture. Indeed, so close was this that the Zapotec even altered the land to emphasize sacred qualities. At Monte Albán, for instance, the entire top of the hill on which they built has been levelled, and all the surrounding hills have been changed and terraced.

41

The volcano Popocatapetl was considered to be the home of important deities who occupied its summit where they waited to receive messages of supplication from the temple priests. Mexico.

The markings on this pottery dish show a jaguar in the centre surrounded by symbols of fire. Such dishes are unlikely to have served any utilitarian function but were probably kept within temple precincts for ritual use. Aztec.

There is also extensive evidence for elaborate underground tombs, many of them containing rich offerings including terracotta urns depicting various deities.

Unfortunately, much of Zapotec writing remains undecipherable and it is therefore impossible to know with certainty which deities and powers were considered to be predominant. One thing we can, however, be fairly certain of is that the ancient gods of agriculture were important. The Maize God and the Rain God, which were of major importance in Aztec culture, must have been known to the Zapotec, as must the Old Fire God, a symbol of the Sun, and on which the world renewal ceremonies were based at the end of a calendrical round of 52 years. We find, too, the Jaguar God as ruler of the Underworld, which stems directly from Olmec belief, as well as an aged Lord of the Underworld who is familiar from Mayan culture under the name of Pauahtun.

Zapotec concern was not entirely with the deities governing the agricultural year or of the Underworld, since various other natural cycles appear as important. Alignments of some of the buildings suggest close observation of astronomical events such as the solstices, equinoxes, and the

Venus cycle (as Morning Star and Evening Star). It is obvious that the Zapotec world was therefore one in which natural patterns and cycles were closely linked with architectural spaces that defined the relationship between people and the deities, and which also created a vertical link between the creative powers of both earth and sky.

Although Zapotec hegemony in Oaxaca never seems to have extended over the early Mixtec settlements, by 1200 AD the Mixtec aristocracy had begun to make serious inroads into areas under Zapotec influence. By a combination of military might and strategically planned 'royal' marriages many of the smaller Zapotec statelets, and finally even Monte Albán itself, came under Mixtec domination, until, eventually, Mixtec-Zapotec populations became so interwoven that little distinction can be made between them. Eventually the Mixtec-Zapotec capital was moved from Monte Albán to Mitla. So confused is this period that we do not know whether Mitla was a Zapotec or Mixtec centre, although the architecture is in a style known as Mixteca-Puebla which is characterized by geometric fretwork patterns on exterior and interior walls, and fret-decorated cruciform tombs which are characteristic of the Mixtec. Despite its architectural identification as Mixtec, legend has it that the Zapotec rulers and nobles are buried in a secret chamber beneath the city. The cultural duality of late Mixtec-Zapotec sites is also reflected in the town of Zaachila, a Zapotec centre with a Zapotec king, but where the tombs are filled with beautiful polychrome pottery that is in the Mixtec style.

While the fortunes of the Mixtec-Zapotec waxed and waned in the Valley of Oaxaca, another powerful influence was gradually emerging in the north, in the Valley of Mexico. Much of the Valley of Mexico had become a cultural wasteland following the fall of the Olmecs, and was, indeed, to remain so for nearly 400 years until the beginning of the Christian era. Throughout this period the area was occupied primarily by small, nomadic groups with some scattered hamlets. Sacred sites within this area were often underground caves, and for some reason which is now obscure one of these became the focus of a local cult. The old Olmec system of honouring the earth and of venturing into the Underworld is apparent again, as is the concept of underground water being especially revered.

The cave is located about 35 miles (56km) north-east of present Mexico City, and has been altered by changing its shape to resemble that of a four-petalled flower, representing the division of the world into four sacred quarters with the spring of origin at its centre. By 300 AD the site of pilgrimage had been enveloped by one of the largest and most powerful city-states in Mexico, that of Teotihuacan. The importance of Teotihuacan is shown by the fact it is known by its Aztec name, meaning 'The Place The Gods Came From', or 'The Place Where The Gods Were Born'. At the height of its power, about 500 AD, Teotihuacan covered an urban area of over 8 sq miles (20 sq km) and had a population that may have been in excess of 200,000. Today it is the most intensively investigated archaeological site in Mexico, as well as the one most frequently visited by tourists.

Most astonishing, perhaps, is that the entire city of Teotihuacan appears to have been carefully planned on a grid pattern that represented the cos-

mos, and that it was built in one single, massive, operation. The influence of this vast metropolis was felt throughout Mesoamerica, and Teotihuacan attracted artisans and traders from far and wide. There was an entire Oaxaca ward here, in which Zapotec potters manufactured their own gray-ware images of the deities, as well as a Mayan ward producing characteristic polychrome pottery. The immensity of this building project, and the care with which it was planned, is seen in the fact that many natural features, such as creeks and hills, were deliberately altered to conform to the overall scheme.

At the heart of Teotihuacan is the gigantic Pyramid of the Sun, with a base equal to that of the Great Pyramid in Egypt and soaring 230ft (70m) high, and the smaller but only slightly less imposing Pyramid of the Moon. They are arranged on the

In addition to skills in astronomy and writing, Mesoamerican cultures demonstrated skilled craftsmanship in working precious metals. The gold pendant shown here bears a design which represents the sun and links the qualities of the metal to the brilliance of the sun.

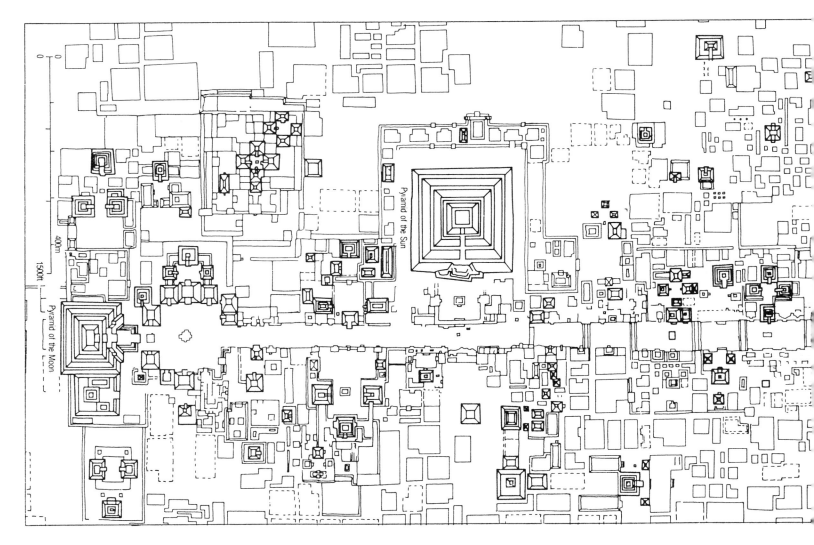

The labels visible on the map:

Pyramid of the Sun

Pyramid of the Moon

The city of Teotihuacan was built to a grid in which the Avenue of the Dead bisected the ceremonial complex at the heart of the city. The drawing shown here has been reconstructed from extensive archaeological investigations at the site. The focus of the ceremonies were the Pyramids of the Sun and Moon, which were surrounded by smaller buildings which functioned as temples and as housing for the nobility.

6,600ft- (2011m) long Avenue of the Dead, with the Pyramid of the Sun on its eastern flank and the Pyramid of the Moon at its northern end. The Avenue of the Dead is itself aligned with the dominant mountain, Cerro Gordo, which forms a magnificent backdrop to the Pyramid of the Moon. Many other alignments are evident. The great stairway of the Pyramid of the Sun, for example, faces a westerly point on the horizon where Tianquitzli (the Pleiades) lies directly in front of it. The significance of this is that the movement of Tianquitzli had direct influence on calculations in the ritual calendar as well as dictating other important events.

Surrounding the Avenue of the Dead are numerous other smaller pyramidal structures, temple complexes, and the houses of the priests and the ruling élite, while beyond these are dense artisan quarters of more modest scale. So far, over 5,000 buildings have been identified here, many of those in the richer élite quarters bearing brilliantly coloured frescoes and relief carvings depicting mythological events. At the Ciudadela (Citadel), which is now thought to have been a royal residence, is, for instance, a large sunken courtyard with the splendid Temple of

Quetzalcoatl at its centre. Relief carvings here depict Feathered Serpents alternating with Fire Serpents, expressing the mythological opposition between these two deities: Feathered Serpent as the god of life and vegetation, and Fire Serpent as the god of heat and the desert. Other buildings have names that reflect the themes of their murals and carvings, such as Palace of the Quetzal Butterfly, or Temple of the Feathered Shells. In the Tepantitla Palace the Teotihuacan conception of the afterworld for those blessed with a watery death is depicted in a riot of dancing figures in a landscape full of flowers and butterflies.

Although we have no written records from Teotihuacan, many of the images that decorate the temples and other buildings are clearly recognizable as deities that were to play an important part in Mayan and Aztec belief. Present are Tlaloc, the Rain God; Chalchiuhtlicue, the Water Goddess; Xipe Totec, or the Flayed Lord, God of Maize; Xochiquetzal, the Goddess of Sexuality; Mictlantecuhltli, the Lord of the Underworld; and, of course, Quetzalcoatl, the Feathered Serpent, and his opposite, the Fire God. Thus at Teotihuacan we

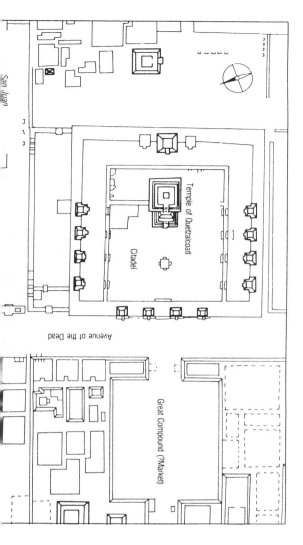

already have in place most of the features that were to become part of the cosmology and mythology of Aztec culture that was extant when the Spanish arrived in the early sixteenth century, and we need to consider Teotihuacan as being the first fully formed Mesoamerican empire.

One question that has puzzled Meso-americanists is the nature of the subsistence base for the great city, since the Valley of Teotihuacan could never have supported such a large population. It now seems probable that the entire Valley of Mexico was brought under *chinampa* (raised field) agricul-ture, in which grid-like plots of land were left by canals cut into lake edges and fertilized by regular applications of mud and pond weed dredged from the canals. This supposition is supported by the dis-covery of *chinampas* in Teotihuacan itself, and the survival of *chinampas* in the Xochimilco area south of Mexico City. The connection between the two is assumed since both have an identical grid pattern. By utilizing such an extensive and amazingly pro-ductive method of growing crops, the population of Teotihuacan would have been well provided for and substantial trade as well as lavish ritual feasts could

have been supported.

But Teotihuacan, like San Lorenzo and La Venta before it, presents us with an altogether more difficult puzzle. Teotihuacan culture lasted only 200 years at its peak, and during the seventh century most of the city was destroyed by fire. We can only guess at what may have happened, but it is apparent that the destruction centred particularly on the élite

Due to the scarcity of water and the reliance on grain crops, the Rain God, Tlaloc, was one of the most powerful deities. Offerings were continually made in attempts to influence Tlaloc and persuade him to send his messengers, the rain clouds. Mixtec.

47

The most impressive feature at Teotihuacan is the massive Pyramid of the Sun. Originally, the pyramid was covered with lime plaster and painted red. Frescoes at the base of the pyramid and covering the walls of the temples depicted mythological events that explained the function and behaviour of the gods.

areas of the city. Could it be that the urban population, ruled over by an oppressive hierarchy of priest-rulers, rose up in an insurrection and destroyed the magnificent buildings that symbolized the divisive nature of Teotihuacan's social order? Another theory is that massive deforestation of the area, caused by burning wood to produce the immense quantity of lime plaster needed to construct the city, may have degraded the environment to such an extent that it was no longer a viable place in which to live.

Legend, however, tells us another story to account for the demise of this great capital city and the significance that Teotihuacan was to have in the later Aztec culture. According to this, a dispute arose between Quetzalcoatl and the evil Tezcatlipoca, or Smoking Mirror. Smoking Mirror, in order to humiliate Quetzalcoatl, plied him with *pulque* (a fermented cactus juice.) While intoxicated, Quetzalcoatl had sexual relations with the Witch Goddess and was forced out of Teotihuacan by Tezcatlipoca. In the bitter fight that erupted during his expulsion, Quetzalcoatl's followers destroyed the city, promising that they would return to reclaim their land.

During the journey towards the Gulf coast, Quetzalcoatl and his retinue of dwarfs and other fantastic creatures founded the city of Tula (Tollan). In his human-god form Quetzalcoatl was established

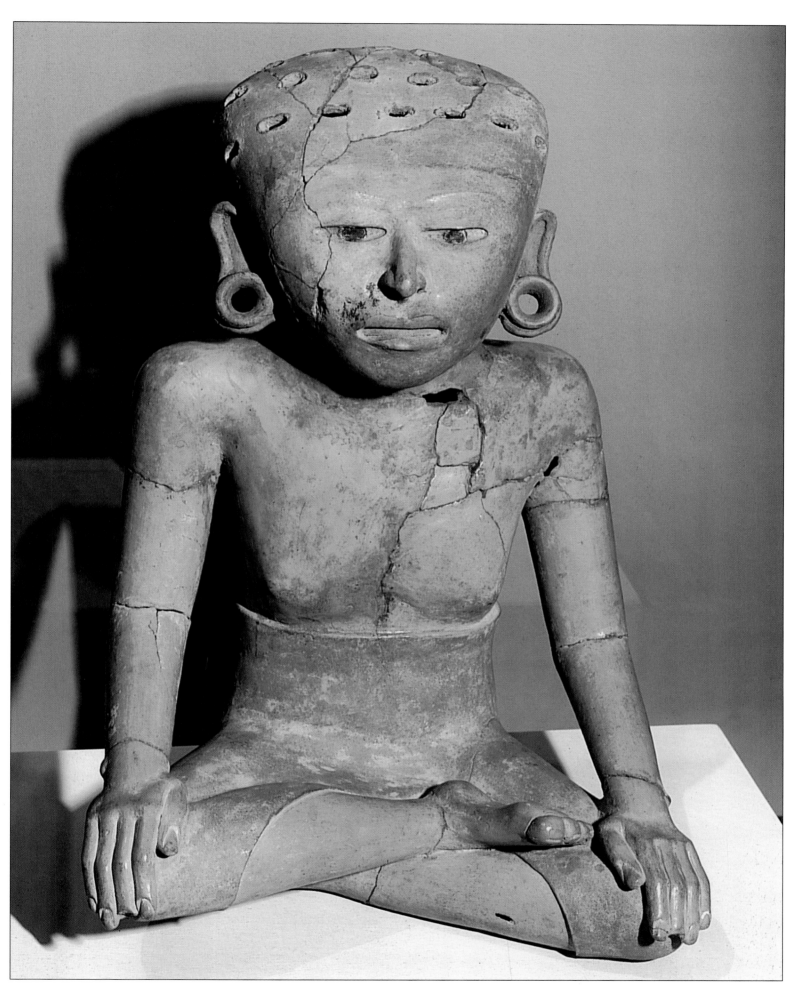

LEFT
Although this has been labelled as a sacrificial stone, the imagery and use of symbols are reminiscent of the Calendar Stone on page 50. The exact function of these types of stone altars is unknown. It is, however, possible that they had both calendrical and sacrificial uses.

OPPOSITE
Masks of noble families were often made to accompany their deceased. Although the function of this mask has not been clearly established, it was recovered from Teotihuacan which the later Aztecs claimed as the ancestral home of their nobility.

here as Topiltzin Quetzalcoatl, Our Young Prince the Feathered Serpent, who was said to have had a miraculous birth and a rigorous training for the priesthood, as well as being a renowned warrior. He was also a reformer, and it is said that he stopped the practice of offering human sacrifices to the deities and instead substituted offerings of fruit, flowers, and butterflies. The enraged Tezcatlipoca, master of sacrificial cults and of offerings of human hearts, sent magic to work against Quetzalcoatl who was forced into exile from Tula. He journeyed further until he reached the Gulf of Mexico, and then disappeared across the waters to the east on a raft of sea serpents, swearing to avenge himself against Tezcatlipoca. It is said he was absorbed into the rising sun, but that his heart continued to shine in a

BELOW
These carvings of warrior figures once supported the roof of the temple on the pyramid dedicated to Quetzalcoatl at the Toltec capital of Tula.

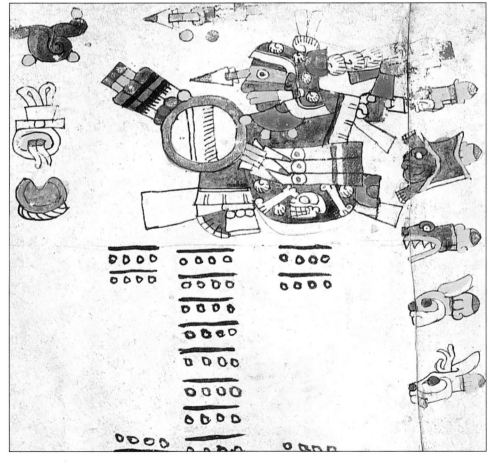

solar eclipse.

More prosaic, but probably more accurate, is that Tula was actually founded about 900 AD by groups of wandering hunter-gathers from two linguistic backgrounds, the Chichimeca and the Toltec, under the leadership of the Chichimeca chieftain Mixcoatl, or Cloud Serpent. This hybrid group – which we now refer to as Toltec – borrowed heavily from other cultures in central Mexico, since we find architectural features that are clearly based on buildings from other earlier sites. The Toltecs were both warriors and traders, and from Tula established a wide sphere of influence that included subject states as well as more peaceful trading stations.

What is definite is that Tula was based on the worship of Quetzalcoatl, since it contains a sizeable temple pyramid dedicated to this deity. It is also apparent that the religious reform credited to Topilitzin Quetzalcoatl may not have been as complete as the legend suggests, since the substructure of the Quetzalcoatl pyramid is adorned with images of the familiar Mesoamerican warrior deities – the Jaguar, Coyote, and Eagle – eating human hearts. If human sacrifice was forbidden at Tula, then this is not indicated in such imagery. It is also belied by the

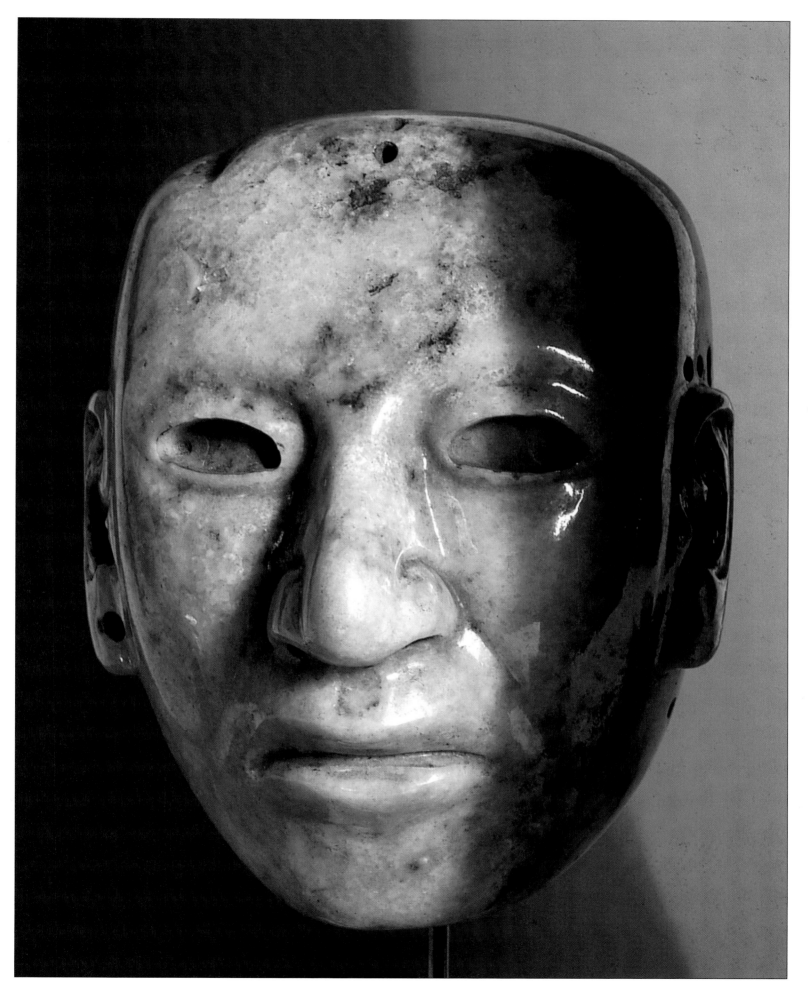

fact that Toltec culture was one of warrior élites, especially of the Jaguar Warriors and Eagle Warriors whose function among the later Aztecs was largely one of obtaining sacrificial human victims. There are also a number of *chacmool* carvings at Tula, which are believed to be sacrificial stones.

Easily the most impressive remains at Tula, and in effect the focal point of the militaristic régime that presided there, are 15ft- (4.6m) high basalt columns erected on the flat platform at the top of the pyramid of Quetzalcoatl and which formerly supported the temple roof. Each of these depicts a Toltec warrior in full military costume, and has the Firebird symbol of the Toltec ruling class shown as a chest ornament. The connection between the warriors and the ruling élite at Tula is thus defined in these figures, since although the warriors are not rulers their status as a highly professional army answerable to the leading members of the city is made patently clear through the carvings and symbols they wear. The power of this army is evident from the Toltec overthrow of the Mayan states in the Yucatán Peninsula of Mexico, since it appears that before 1200 AD the Toltec had virtually depopulated the countryside and concentrated the Mayan nobility as hostages in the city of Chichén Itzá, which was largely rebuilt by Mayan labour under Toltec direction.

By 1224 AD, however, Toltec power had waned and all that remained of the empire were the ruined ceremonial centres and the legends of Topilitzin Quetzalcoatl, of a race of giants that was said to have built Teotihuacan, and of a Toltec past in which it was stated the buildings themselves were covered with jewels, that all knowledge flowed from their capital city of Tula, and that it was the Toltecs at Tula who invented the ritual calendar and writing systems of Mesoamerica. As we have seen, much of this was fantastic embellishment of fact, since the calendar and writing, at least in a rudimentary form, had been present in Mesoamerica since the late Olmec period of some 2,000 years earlier. Nevertheless, the Toltec rulers were held in such esteem as the personification of Quetzalcoatl, that Aztec rulers claimed Toltec lineage as determining their own rights to powerful status as divine priest-kings.

LEFT
Details of Toltec warrior costume can be clearly seen in this view of the carved roof supports from the Pyramid of Quetzalcoatl at Tula.

PAGE 54
TOP
Detail of a polychrome mural showing a jaguar. The jaguar is blowing into a conch shell which was used as a horn both by warriors in battle and by priests during rituals.

BELOW
This image of a warrior depicts Tezcatlipoca who was associated with the direction north. When comming from this direction he brought darkness, danger and death. This is symbolized on his robe by the decorations of a skull and other human bones.

PAGE 55
Although this small jade head has not been clearly identified, the small hole on the forehead suggests that it was pierced for the attachment of a thong and that it was probably worn as a pendant. Aztec.

CHAPTER THREE
THE MAYA: HEROIC ANCESTORS
OF THE AZTECS

Contemporary with the emergence in the north of the great empire of Teotihuacan, parallel developments in the southern parts of Mesoamerica heralded the rise of the Maya. Although the Maya were for long presented as a unified confederacy of states, it is now known that there was actually very little political cohesion between the different groups and that much of Maya life was marked by conflicts between competitive rather than cooperative neighbours. It is even emerging that the cultural uniformity of Maya architecture and belief has at least two clear expressions: that of the lowlands of the Petén-Yucatán Peninsula, and that of the highlands of Chiapas and Guatemala. In fact, the 'typical' Maya sites of the Classic period, from before 300 AD until about 900 AD, which are characterized by huge stucco-covered temple-pyramids, complex multi-roomed palaces, causeways connecting buildings (and, at times, running between cities), ball courts, true writing, and monumental stelae bearing inscriptions, are all in the lowland regions of the Petén-Yucatán Peninsula. By contrast, the highland Classic Maya in Chiapas and Guatemala seem to have built little stone architecture and to have had only rare recourse to recording their achievements in written records.

In common with so many of the Mesoamerican cultures, that of the Maya has its beginnings with relatively unsophisticated local groups who, although possessing a distinctive culture of their own, nevertheless owed a debt to the ancient civilization of the Olmec. Some scholars even claim that the Maya are direct descendants of the Olmec, but the apparent gap in continuity from the demise of the Olmec in 400 BC to the beginnings of Mayan culture at the start of the Christian era make it difficult to trace any direct relationships. More spectacular – and, in fact, on a par with the rapid development of Teotihuacan in the north – was the sudden efflorescence of Maya art and architecture between its incipient stages and the first massive city-states they started to build about 200 AD. From simple river-cobble-covered earthen mounds at Itzapa on the Pacific plain of Chiapas, Maya culture reached its 'Classic' period within a mere 200 years. Part of this development and the spread of Maya ideology throughout the southern regions of Mesoamerica has been traced back to Kaminaljuyú, a now destroyed site on the western outskirts of Guatemala City, which contained several hundred great pyramid mounds, and to El Mirador which contained stucco-covered pyramids 230ft (70m) in height.

The Maya did not, of course, develop in isolation from other expressions of the Mesoamerican peoples. Kaminaljuyú shows strong influence from Teotihuacan, to the extent that much of its later architecture was rebuilt to Teotihuacan ideals and proportions, and it is clear it functioned as part of the great Teotihuacan empire that influenced virtually all of Mesoamerica. Teotihuacan influence must, however, also have been felt in the Petén, since early structures at Tikal and Uaxactún indicate this. Such

structures are now buried beneath later Maya temple structures in layers of rebuilding that occurred with the internment of élite members of the Maya aristocracy. The Teotihuacan influence is further indicated by carvings discovered at these sites, such as that of a Maya ruler found at Tikal who is flanked by two warriors wearing characteristic Teotihuacan costume.

But this influence, undoubtedly stemming from a Teotihuacan warrior-merchant class, was not destined to last. By 534 AD it was over and all of Mesoamerica was thrown into turmoil. No new buildings or monuments were erected during the next 60 years. After this, however, presumably no longer under restraints from the north, Maya culture in the lowlands flourished and grew with unprece-

This lintel from the Mayan city of Yaxchilan is marked with glyphs which are carved in relief to represent a date. This was usually the date on which a building had been completed. The date recorded here is 11 February, 526 AD.

arrival of the Spanish *conquistadores*.

It is, then, from the period roughly between 200 AD and 900 AD that we need to consider Classic Maya culture, and particularly as expressed in the lowland areas of the Petén-Yucatán tropical forest. Many of the deities we have already mentioned are familiar ones: Feathered Serpent, the Rain God, the Old God of Fire, the Jaguar and Eagle, and so on, are all well represented in Maya culture. We are familiar from earlier periods with the close relationship between space and time, and with astronomical alignments in the architectural layouts of the massive pyramid- and temple-dominated centres; although those of the Maya were never planned on the strict grid techniques of Teotihuacan. And once again, we also find an hierarchy of élite priest-rulers, plus the use of calendrical notation and a system of writing. Among the Maya, however, all of these were brought to heights of refinement that were unique anywhere in the New World.

Pre-eminent among these developments was the refinement of the Maya script; the only system of writing in the ancient New World by which an entire language could be expressed, using elements drawn both from ideographs and from phonetics. Thus the Maya were able to make statements about ideas as well as express the sounds of the language, and, often, they combined the two. Literally hundreds of stelae, carvings, paintings, and so forth are known from the Classic period. With advances in our knowledge over the past 25 years, it is now possible to decipher most of these. The texts refer to the dynastic activities of the ruling élites and are dated using the 'Maya' calendar (which, of course, the Maya did not invent, since it is suspected that calendrical notation was already becoming important in late Olmec culture).

Because many of these ruling élites were closely associated with the deities of the Maya world, we have a wealth of data from which we can begin to understand the beliefs and ideals of the Classic period. There are also records of Maya astronomical observations. From these we know they kept watch on the cycles of the sun and moon, and of planets such as Venus, Jupiter, Mars, and Mercury, which they were able to calculate with astonishing accuracy. For example, the Maya calculated the synodic period of the planet Venus to be 584 days: less than a single decimal point short of the calculations of modern scientists. They were also able to predict eclipses of the sun to within less than seven minutes of the modern value. Although the Maya used these calculations and measurements for astrological

dented vigour. During this period literally hundreds of pyramids, palaces, temples, causeways, and urban settlements were created. It is obvious from the archaeological evidence that the Maya in the Classic period had massive ceremonial centres supported by urban populations that numbered in their thousands. Then suddenly, in the tenth century, Maya civilization collapsed. The ancient and beautiful city and ceremonial centres they had constructed were abandoned and left to ruin, and the Maya returned to living as small-scale farmers and fishermen until the rather than astronomical purposes, we should nevertheless consider their achievements as a true science.

Yet despite the grandeur and technological achievements of the Maya, very little was known about them until recently. Not until the publication of their discoveries in the 1840s by John Lloyd Stephens, a gifted amateur archaeologist, and Frederick Catherwood, an artist, was any real interest expressed. Of the hundreds of Maya centres in existence only three archaeological sites were actually known from the Maya area prior to Stephens' and Catherwood's revelations: these were Copán, in Honduras; Palenque, in Chiapas; and Uxmal, in the Yucatán. Not only that, but no one had by then identified these sites as Mayan, since the Maya of the

time were considered to be small und uneducated tribal groups whose members were primarily employed to work the haciendas of rich landowners. Stephens and Catherwood discovered numerous sites throughout the Maya area, including large temple complexes that were frequently located only a few miles from one another, and also noted that these were built by the 'Old Ones': the ancestors of the contemporary Maya.

Part of this paucity of information was due to dense tropical vegetation covering many of the complexes. Stephens tells us of investigating the upper terrace on the summit of one pyramid for an entire day and being totally unaware of another adjacent building because of the density of the trees and

Carved pendant depicting a Mayan ruler from the city of Copán. He is wearing a typical Chac-xib-chac *headdress which indicates status given by the gods.*

shrubs. His line of vision was so obscured by tropical growth that he was unable to discern a major construction at even so small a distance. In all his reports he recalls hiring local people to hack a path to the sites with machetes, and notes that many of the indigenous populations were unaware of the presence of local ruins other than those in the vicinity of their cleared *milpas*, or maize fields.

Even the known archaeological sites had been but poorly investigated. When Stephens and Catherwood arrived at Copán, after an exhausting trek through thick brush that had to be cleared inch by inch by their guides, they found the site covered with jungle growth. This was the 'Lost Civilization' of the Maya, buried deep in the Honduran jungle, and which no stretch of the nineteenth-century imagination could link to the contemporary world of the Indians. Stephens wrote in his journal, after clambering up several tree- and shrub-covered Copán pyramids:

We sat down on the very edge of the wall and strove in vain to penetrate the mystery by which we were surrounded. Who were the people that build this city? In the ruined cities of Egypt, even in long-lost Petra, the stranger knows the story of the people whose vestiges are around him. America, say historians, was peopled by savages: but savages never reared these structures, savages never carved these stones ... There were no associations connected with the place: none of those stirring recollections which hallow Rome, Athens, and 'the world's great mistress' on the Egyptian plains: but architecture, sculpture, and painting, all the arts which embellished life, had flourished in this overgrown forest: orators, warriors and statesment, beauty, ambition and glory had lived and passed away, and none knew that such things had been, or could tell of their past existence. (John L Stephens: Incidents of Travel in Central America. London, *1844, pp.82-83).*

The full wealth of Maya culture was not only

OPPOSITE
Mayan architecture was often elaborately embellished with depictions of the deity to whom the building was dedicated. The façade from one of the buildings of the Nunnery quadrangle at Uxmal is carved to represent the Rain God, Chac.

BELOW
The so-called Pyramid of the Magician at Uxmal is a good example of Mayan monumental architecture.

63

hidden from mid-nineteenth-century explorers. It was not realized until well into the twentieth century, and our knowledge of the complexity and richness of these cultures is continually expanding. We now know, for example, that the various Maya states were almost continually at war, with the capture of leading nobles as sacrificial victims from neighbouring centres their prime objective. Many stelae give the name and date of the capture and ritual execution of such rulers, presumably as a means of gaining political rather than territorial control. In this respect we need to remember that the priest-rulers were considered to be incarnations of the deities. By destroying a neighbouring ruler, those of an adjoining centre effectively demonstrated their success in a cosmological battle: one between their own ruling deity and that of their neighbours. Because of this it is impossible to separate myth from fact, and it is unlikely that the ancient Maya made any such distinction: to them, any activity was a representation of their mythological beliefs and ideology, and the world of the gods and of the people was an inseparable one.

Such a world-view is very evident in the magnificent murals discovered at the Maya centre of Bonampak, on a tributary of the Usumacinta river system. These were discovered in 1946 and can be dated by the Maya calendar to soon after 800 AD. They tell a simple narrative: a battle, its consequences, and the victory that followed. But revealed within this is an amazing story of Maya warfare. We see splendidly dressed Maya warriors from Bonampak setting off against their enemies through the dense undergrowth of a tropical forest, accompanied by musicians who are blowing war trumpets of wood and bark. Then we see the prisoners, stripped

an underground passage. By 1952, after careful and arduous work that required the removal of several tons of rubble from a steep interior staircase leading from the top of the pyramid through its centre and down to ground level, Ruz entered a small crypt which served as the tomb of the Maya king Pacal (Lord Shield), who had allegedly ruled Palenque for 68 years until his death in 683 AD. Unlike most Mayan burials this had not been desecrated. In the centre was Pacal's sarcophagus, still containing his remains covered with remnants of a jade mask, necklaces, ear spools, rings, and mother-of-pearl ornaments. Reliefs of stucco covered the walls, and the floor was littered with pottery vessels, carved portrait heads, and the skeletons of five sacrificial victims.

The most revealing part of the tomb, however, was the elaborate sarcophagus lid. Measuring 12 ft x 7 ft (3.6m x 2m), this was carved to depict the Maya vision of the cosmos and of Pacal's movement through it. The imagery included a fantastic tree bedecked with jewels, mirrors, and blood-letting bowls, with a celestial bird perched on top. Also shown is Pacal, falling backwards into Xibalba, the Underworld, through the gaping jaws of two skeletal serpents. Once again we see in this powerful imagery a concern to link the Sky, Earth, and Underworld powers and of the movement of Sacred Beings through the three levels of the cosmos. But we also find the idea of an existence beyond that of the living, since after the crypt was sealed the small, hollow, stairway of stone slabs that Ruz discovered was laid to facilitate Pacal's communication between the Lower and Upper worlds. In addition, the sides of the sarcophagus bore carvings depicting Pacal's ancestors rising from the branches of other cosmic trees. Thus the tomb acted not only as a burial place for Pacal, but also as a centre through which Pacal and his ancestors could be regenerated.

Part of this regenerative idea in Maya belief has to be understood in terms of the cosmic tree that features so prominently in Pacal's tomb and also at other ceremonial buildings throughout Palenque. In this respect we need to remember the Maya world was one of tropical forest and jungle, in which vegetation played an overwhelming role. We can only imagine the immense amount of labour and time that went into clearing spaces in the jungle to erect the ceremonial centres and causeways, and the stunning impression the monumental buildings made against their backdrop of tropical growth. The pyramids and other buildings, with their white lime plaster, relief carvings, and brilliantly coloured paintings of Maya myths and history were intended to be viewed

of their regal clothing – presumably to exclude them from any identification with their own deities – and being tortured by having their fingernails drawn out. Elsewhere there is a noble captive, sprawled across the steps of Bonampak's pyramid, with a severed head lying nearby. Over all this presides a lord dressed as a Jaguar Warrior, attended by ladies clad in white robes who are offering sacrificial penance by drawing cords knotted with thorns through their tongues.

Other revelations come from Palenque, a lowland Maya site built on wooded hills overlooking alluvial plains which stretch toward the Gulf of Mexico, where inscriptions record the reign of a royal family from the fourth century AD until the decline of the capital in the late nineth century. Our knowledge of this is due largely to the work of Alberto Ruz, who, in 1949, deduced that the floor of the rear hall of the Temple of Inscriptions concealed

against the dense greens of the tropics. Just as the forest itself was in a continual process of regeneration and growth, so too was the symbol of the cosmic tree from Pacal's tomb. The same symbol is used in the sanctuaries placed within the Temple of the Cross and the Temple of the Foliated Cross, where a branching world-tree is depicted with the figure of the quetzal bird above it.

The importance of vegetation also has to be considered from the point of view that the Maya were an agricultural people, dependent for their subsistence on the *milpas* (maize fields) that surrounded the residential areas of their great centres. Agriculture was the essential life-force of the Maya and seen as a sacred activity. We should bear in mind here that vegetation was created before humans and the first people were created by the gods from maize. Just as the seeds of maize would sprout and mature in a sacred manner, so, too, would the seeds of people sprout and mature under the auspices of the gods and goddesses of vegetation, growth, and fertility. We can take this idea even further and make it more explicit by referring to the image of the sacred tree in the Temple of the Foliated Cross. This tree rises from the Underworld, the abode of the ancestors, and is formed from a composite of the four sacred trees that depict the world directions. It is transformed into a maize plant which, instead of bearing ears of corn, bears the heads of young men whose beauty, to the Maya, was like that of ripe maize.

When viewed in this way, the symbolism of Pacal's sarcophagus becomes much clearer. As the priest-king he was the embodiment of the sacred tree, the *axis mundi* of the Maya world, who originates with the ancestors and who will return with his descendants, all of whom ripen and grow to maturity as the maize ripens and grows. In a similar manner, the Sun was thought to descend into the Underworld each evening and to be reborn at dawn, and this symbol is also depicted in Pacal's tomb – it is, in fact, intrinsically linked with Pacal since it forms part of his throne – and is also present at the other temples in association with the cosmic tree. Maya myth tells us further that the tree was created first, and that in a dispute between the gods of the Underworld and the Sacred Twins the Twins were defeated and their decapitated heads placed on a tree, from which sprouted maize. From this we must understand that a priest-ruler such as Pacal was not merely a king, in our sense of the word, but a symbol of cosmic order. It was through him that the sacred world of the gods was brought into the presence of and aligned with the social world of the people. It was also through him that the creative powers of the Upper, Middle, and Lower Worlds were united.

Pacal's descent into the Underworld through the jaws of the skeletal serpents must also relate to the emergence of the Feathered Serpent from the Underworld through the jaws of the Jaguar God we

LEFT
The decoration on the rim of this vase is composed from date glyphs, and there are also glyphs above the painted figures. The figures are dressed as warriors in elaborate costumes and masks.

PAGE 70
This finely modelled and realistic stucco head from Palenque is reputed to be a portrait of Pacal who claimed leadership through direct descent from the Earth Mother deity.

PAGE 71
This elaborately decorated building from the Toltec-Maya site of Chichén Itzá is generally referred to as La Iglesia, *'The Church', although the exact function of the building is not known. Of interest, however, are the projecting carvings, on the corners and in the centre of each face of the building, which indicate that it had some connection with Rain God.*

71

Feathered Serpent, emerges again as the patron deity of Mesoamerican priest-rulers, and is linked with the Jaguar. The link is further emphasized on a wooden lintel carved to represent the inauguration of the Tikal king, Ah Cacau, on which Ah Cacau is shown seated on a throne in front of a gigantic Jaguar protector.

We should note, too, that Maya rulers were regarded as Mah K'ina (Great Sun Lord), as well as Ahau (Lord) which was used to mark a significant date in the Mayan calendar. There is a clear correlation between the Sun, the ritual calendar, and the status of an important ruler which tends to confirm the relationship between the ruler and the deities. The link with Quetzalcoatl is also confirmed when we consider the ceremonial dress of rulers on state occasions. Various stelae depict famous rulers, such as Smoke Jaguar, Yax Pac (First Dawn), Kakukpacal (Fire is his Shield), Shield Jaguar, and Two-Legged Jaguar. The only consistent element in all these depictions is the fabulous headdress of quetzal feathers, although all are adorned with various other symbols of status that represent the presence of the divinities. Arrayed in such costumes the priest-rulers appeared as more than human. They had a sacred presence that referred to the myths and gods, and which was represented in their dress.

The power of such leaders is unquestioned: as representatives of the deities they controlled forces that no other human being could even begin to think of acquiring. Such power came from the ancestors,

considered in relation to Olmec belief. Just as Feathered Serpent was born from the Jaguar guardians of the Underworld, so the priest-ruler returns to the Underworld via the intercession of the Serpent who protects him from the Jaguar deities. Here we need to remember that Jaguars and Eagles were the warrior élite, and were therefore the protectors of their own priest-rulers but also a threat to the leaders of other communities. It was their responsibility to depose the priest-rulers of rival centres and to present them as sacrificial victims in the continual struggles for supremacy that took place between the different Maya states. Thus Quetzacoatl, the and without ancestral privilege it was impossible for anyone to aspire to such an exalted position. Thus the Maya leaders were members of royal lineages in which a son (and very occasionally a daughter) inherited his position at the death of his father. But power also brought responsibility, since the priest-rulers of the Mayan world were held directly responsible for the well-being of the community. Failure to carry out prescribed ceremonies in the correct manner could bring disaster, and the blame might be laid at the feet of the priest-ruler. The reign of any priest-ruler was therefore subject to tensions and uncertainty, and Pacal, who is reputed to have ruled successfully from the age of 12 until his death at 81, is an exception. Many stelae suggest that priest-rulers more often had short careers, and that warfare – which as we have seen often had as its goal the capture and sacrifice of a neighbouring priest-ruler – was a major factor in the development of the complex Maya societies. A complete record of the suc-

This commemorative stela from Piedras Negras records the rulership of a Mayan leader named Two Wind. The detail shown here indicates Two Wind's more aggressive aspect since it depicts his warrior's jaguar mask.

These realistic figurines from the island of Jaina depict a richly attired couple of dignitaries in full regalia. Note especially the circular pendant worn by the man and the similar disk held by the woman, which are referred to as 'mirrors' and were symbols of authority.

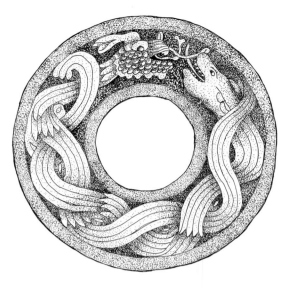

cession of 39 kings at Tikal suggests the average rule was only about 12 years.

It also follows that a city without a ruler was in a state of what could be called 'suspended animation'. The loss of a ruler effectively removed the essential link between this world and the supernatural, which was seen by the Maya as necessary to normal everyday life. In other words, the supernatural sanction and motivation for all activities, whether political, economic, military, or ritual, was removed by the capture or death of the priest-ruler. Even such

a powerful city as Tikal, which is the largest known Maya centre and has a core of monumental buildings covering an area of 6 sq miles (16 sq km) was thrown into a depression that lasted over a century when the smaller city of Caracol captured and sacrificed Tikal's ruler, Double Bird. After Double Bird's overthrow much of Tikal's wealth was diverted as tribute to Caracol, and while Tikal declined Caracol grew in power and strength.

In common with Mayan ideology, the inauguration of their priest-rulers was not simply a matter of direct accession to the throne, but was governed by cosmology and made on significant calendrical dates that provided auspicious omens for future prosperity. Tikal's recovery, for instance, was made under Ah Cacau, who was enthroned exactly 13 *katuns* (256 years) after the accession of a previously successful ruler, Stormy Sky; the reason being that 13 signified a complete calendrical round of *katuns* and signified the beginning of a new era. It is also likely that Pacal's 'birth-date' was actually chosen to coincide with the mythical birth-date of the First Mother, the mother of the gods. This assertion is implied by the fact that Pacal's apparent lengthy reign may be fictitious, since initial study of the skeleton suggests it is that of a male aged about 40 rather than the 81 years stated in the glyphs. It is also significant that the name of Pacal's mother, Lady Zac Kuk (White Macaw), who had ruled Palenque before him, was written with the glyph for the First Mother. It therefore appears that Pacal's birth-date was chosen for him as an assertion of his divine right to rule rather than being the actual date of his birth.

There is also evidence that Mayan architecture was planned according to cosmological beliefs as well as with particular astronomical alignments. One of the temple courtyards at Palenque, for

instance, contains three temples mounted on a rectangular raised platform. These are the Temple of the Cross at the northern side, on a platform which raises it higher than the other buildings; the Temple of the Sun at the west; and the Temple of the Foliated Cross at the east. The arrangement into four is a symbol of the four sacred directions, but the symbolism goes much deeper than this. We should note that there are buildings on only three sides of the rectangle, representing the trinity of Upper, Middle, and Lower worlds. The northern building is raised higher in accordance with the important celestial associations made with north in Mayan cosmology, and, as mentioned above, bears murals depicting the sacred world tree, or *axis mundi*, of Mayan belief. The Temple of the Sun is decorated with images of the Jaguar patron of the Underworld and is appropriately at west, the direction associated with the setting sun, death, and the blood of ritual sacrifice. East, the place of the rising sun and of maize and growth, is in acordance with Mayan ideals of the Sun and Maize

as life-givers and, therefore, it is appropriate for the Temple of the Foliated Cross, that is, of growth and vegetation, to be located here. The fourth, open, side points in the direction of emptiness and midnight; a period when the Sun is considered to be dead in Xibalba. In addition, the presence of carvings of *witz* masks identify the temples with the Sacred Mountain, and the centre rear room of each, in which the murals are painted, is a *pib na*, or representation of the Underworld.

Thus Mayan myths and cosmology are expressed in the person of the priest-ruler, in the dates associated with major events, as well as in the placement of architectural features. In this sense we can say that perhaps the most commanding thing in Maya life was a predictable structure or order related to the natural and the supernatural, to the succession of the noble élites, the management of economic, political, military, and ritual life, as well as in architecture. But in order for there to be structure and order there needs to be a basis on which it is

This photograph shows the pyramid at Chichén Itzá that was dedicated to Kukulcan, one of the guises of Quetzalcoatl. The temple on the top of the pyramid is dedicated to Quetzalcoatl, and was a focus for ritual activities that celebrated the cult of Feathered Serpent.

and Xbalanque, were important deities who help to explain one extraordinary aspect of Mayan life: the ritual ball game. Hunapa and Xbalanque represent, respectively, the Sun (symbol of life and celestial power) and the Jaguar (the deity of the Underworld and Death). From this we already see a duality in Mayan thinking, as well as a link between the powers of life and death. The myth tells us that the fathers of the Twins, also twins, had been expert ball-players, and as a result they were invited to Xibalba (the Underworld – symbolically meaning they had died) where they were defeated and sacrificed by the Lords of the Dead, each of whom bore the name of a malignant or infectious disease. One of the Twins was buried beneath the ball-court at Xibalba, the other was decapitated and his head hung in a tree. From here he spat into the hand of Lady Blood, the daughter of Ek Chuuah, the God of the Merchants who has Underworld connections, and impregnated her. In fear of her life, Lady Blood fled to the earth to escape her angry father where she gave birth to the Twin Heroes.

Like their fathers before them the Twin Heroes became expert ball-players, but this time they defeated the Lords of Death. Finally the Twins sacrificed themselves by fire, but were reborn and returned to Xibalba where they astonished the gods by decapitating one another and then restoring themselves to life. When the Death Gods requested they perform this trick on them, they decapitated two of the Gods, One Death and Seven Death, but left them dead and extracted promises from the others to do no more harm. After this they became the primary celestial bodies, the Sun and Venus (as Morning and Evening Star), who each day re-enact their journey from Xibalba at dawn and their return there in the evening.

This tale demonstrates a number of basic principles in Maya thought: that extraordinary humans can travel to Xibalba and return; that rebirth after death is possible; and that rebirth is only achieved through sacrifice (the Twins are sacrificed both by fire and by decapitation). The ball-court, a ubiquitous feature in all Mesoamerican cultures, therefore becomes the threshold between the human world and Xibalba, and the game that was played there was a ritual re-enactment of the confrontation between the Twin Heroes and the Lords of the Dead. In another sense, of course, the game represents the ordering of time through the movements of the Sun and Venus, as well as the fates of people that are dependent on this. Interpretation of murals depicting the ball game suggest that the ball was actually considered to be a symbol of the Sun.

founded, and in the Mayan world this, essentially, was time. More specifically, it was based on what the Maya knew as the Sky Wanderers: the sun, moon, planets, and stars that mark the passage of time. Although the movements of these were carefully observed and recorded by the Maya priest-astronomers, we must also bear in mind that to the Maya they were not only readily observable celestial bodies but also deities. Time, therefore, was given by the gods, and in order to propitiate the gods and ensure the structures they gave were maintained sacrifices and rituals were demanded.

Among these gods the Twin Heroes, Hunapa

The game itself was played with a hard rubber ball by two opposing teams wearing protective clothing consisting of a wide, heavy belt of wood and leather, kneepads, hip-pads, gloves, and sometimes, even helmets. It was hard and fast, although deceptively simple. The principle was to pass the ball through one of two stone rings set high on the walls on the long sides of the ball-court, using hips, elbows, or knees to propel the ball. We would be wrong to consider the ball game merely as a demonstration of athletic prowess. It was an intensely serious ritual act played by teams from noble families of opposing centres, and was played within a court that was, in effect, a cosmological diagram. The imagery of death and sacrifice was prevalent, and at the end of the game the captain of the losing side was sacrificed by decapitation; thus emulating the precedent set by the Twin Heroes. Some scholars give a slightly different interpretation by suggesting it was the captain of the winning team who was willingly sacrificed as a ritual honour; thereby ensuring himself a place in the first level of Xibalba, the Maya equivalent of paradise.

In order to understand the Maya practice of human sacrifice and of personal offerings of blood, we need to remember that the people were created in order that they should be able to name the gods and praise them. Thus there exists a reciprocal relationship between the people and the gods: the gods nurture the people, but demand that the people also nurture them. Both the people and the gods are thus dependent beings, and part of the means of respecting, praising, and calling the gods into the social world was by blood-letting. The presence of the gods was, of course, crucial at any major event, such as the accession of a new ruler, the dedication of a new temple, or on days marked as particularly auspicious in the ritual calendar, and it was on occasions such as this that human sacrifice was demanded. Personal blood-letting by a priest-ruler was understood as the personal blood-letting of the deity the ruler represented. Thus to the Maya the idea of sacrifice was also reciprocated.

The reciprocal sacrifice of the gods is further apparent in the daily descent into Xibalba, or death, of the celestial bodies, as well as in the periodic death and rebirth of other deities such as Maize. When we consider that each deity is also a dual character with the power of giving and withholding life, the sacrifices become even clearer. Thus the Sun, although named as a life-giver, is also the bringer of searing heat which can destroy the crops. Chac, the Rain God, can similarly bring life-giving rain but can also hold it back. At the same time each deity had four aspects associated with the four directions, and as we have already seen these four directions represent two of life – the rising Sun and Vegetation – and two of death – the setting Sun and the dead Sun. To the Maya the worlds of the living and the dead were inextricably linked. Life demanded death so there could be rebirth and rejuvenation, and without this the structured order of the Maya world would disintegrate and throw everything into chaos.

We should not, of course, consider the Maya rituals as a continual round of human sacrifice. The decapitation of victims, cutting out of hearts, or throwing of people into the sacred wells, or *cenotes*, occurred only at periods of tremendous importance and of famine or pestilence. It is also apparent that men, women, and children were sacrificed in more or less equal numbers. Personal blood-letting was far more frequent, both among the noble families and among those of lower status, and accompanied any personal misfortune and/or change in an individual's circumstances. In a sense the blood formed part of any rite of passage, such as a birth, marriage, or death, by inviting a deity to look favourably on the individual concerned. The most frequent offerings, however, were those of animals, precious objects (particularly of jade), and of food and flowers. By far the greater majority of the population were only ever spectators at the human offerings, implying again that it was the noble élite who had the responsibility of bearing the pain of blood-letting and the obligation of conducting the rituals in which blood was given to the gods.

THE FINAL PHASE: AZTEC DOMINATION

The final phase in Mesoamerican history began in 1325 AD with the founding of the city of Tenochtitlan and the establishment of the Aztec empire in the Valley of Mexico. By this time the great capital city of Teotihuacan had been in ruins for nearly 600 years, Mayan power in the lowlands had been waning for 400 years and their cities lay deserted and destroyed: the Toltec capital of Tula had been razed about 100 years earlier. All the great cultures had risen, peaked, and then fallen into decline, and a virtual civil war raged throughout much of the Mesoamerican area. The Valley of Mexico in particular, although still relatively populous, was settled by numerous small city-states which were constantly at war with one another or involved in complicated, and often short-lived, political alliances. The pattern of Mesoamerican disintegration that followed the fall of Teotihuacan was, therefore, being repeated in the Valley of Mexico with the collapse of the centralized authority and control that the Toltecs had exercised from Tula.

In the early thirteenth century, when the Chichimeca ancestors of the Aztec first entered the area as nomadic hunters and warriors, the Valley of Mexico was all that remained of the ill-fated Toltec empire. Only a few families of royal lineage still exerted any authority, and these only over small towns when compared with the once great cities. But proud blood still ran in the Toltec veins and the Chichimeca (so named because the Valley people were unable to understand their speech and felt all they ever said was 'chi-chi-chi', meaning something

unintelligible) were regarded as barbarians by the city-dwellers. The principal Valley settlements were those of the Tepanec in the north-west, Texcoco in the east, and Colhuacan to the south. The divisive state into which they had fallen was reflected in the fact that each town had its own patron deity. Over all, however, was the memory of the furious Tezcatlipoca, or Smoking Mirror, who had brought about the downfall of the Feathered Serpent, Quetzalcoatl, from his position as the principal deity.

The Chichimeca, at first, served as mercenary warriors to any one of the states involved in these conflicts, finally becoming subject themselves to the powerful forces present at Colhuacan, where the rulers claimed direct descent from the Toltec lineages from Tula and thus still ruled under the divine inspiration of Quetzalcoatl. During these trials the Aztec ancestors undoubtedly gained considerable knowledge of the military tactics of all the rival

states. Through military valour, intrigue, and carefully arranged marriages – including marriages with the remnant ruling families of the Toltecs in order to gain divine sanction for their own rulers – the Chichimeca gradually increased in strength, until, having had the audacity to sacrifice the daughter of a leading family of Colhuacan, they were banished to the islands of the great lake that filled the Valley of Mexico.

This fulfilled the visions of the Chichimeca priests, for it was said that after many years of privation and wandering as a punishment for their sins they would find a lake full of islands, on one of which an eagle – the symbol of Tezcatlipoca – rested on a *nopal* cactus. This was to be the site of the Aztec capital of Tenochtitlan, from where they would rise to a position of dominance over all others. Significantly, the vision came to the Chichimeca priests via Tezcatlipoca in his guise as Huitzilopochtli, and it was therefore to Huitzilopochtli that the girl from Colhuacan had been sacrificed in the divine 'marriage' that drove the Chichimeca into exile and to the site that would become the capital of the vast and powerful Aztec empire.

Whatever they may have lacked in refinement in comparison with their more sophisticated city neighbours, the Chichimeca more than compensated for it by their determination, courage, pride, and tireless spirit. The swampy marshlands to which they had been banished held little promise, but the Chichimeca managed to survive there and to gradually increase in strength and influence. As their power grew the rulers of Tenochtitlan began to reclaim land and to build the first stages of their capital. They formed an alliance with and then overthrew another Chichimeca settlement, Tepanec, which helped consolidate their position, following which they formed the Triple Alliance of Tenochtitlan, Texcoco, and Tlacopan. These are the people we now know as Aztec, which is derived from Axatlan: the legendary place from which the Chichimeca migrations are said to have begun in the lands of Mictla, the Country of the Dead.

During their earlier wanderings the Aztec had acquired not only military knowledge, but had also subsumed much other Mesoamerican belief into their own world of animistic deities. We saw previously that Tezcatlipoca, who was to become the Aztec patron deity, was the evil twin brother of Quetzalcoatl and had been responsible for driving Quetzalcoatl into exile. As the War God it was he who directed the Aztec in the conquest of other nations, but he is a far more complex character than this as is reflected in another of his names, Titlauacan, 'He Who Is Closest To The Shoulder'. In other words, the god who stands closest to one's shoulder whispering thoughts of violence and trickery.

It is appropriate to the Aztec that Tezcatlipoca should be adopted as a patron, since he gave authority to warriors and to war leaders and it was by conquest and the subjugation of neighbouring peoples that the Aztec empire was built. It was also due to the excesses of Tezcatlipoca, which drove the Aztec to similar excess, that they have gained a place in history which links them so closely to acts of widespread human sacrifice and occasional ritual cannibalism. In fact, everything about Tezcatlipoca in his

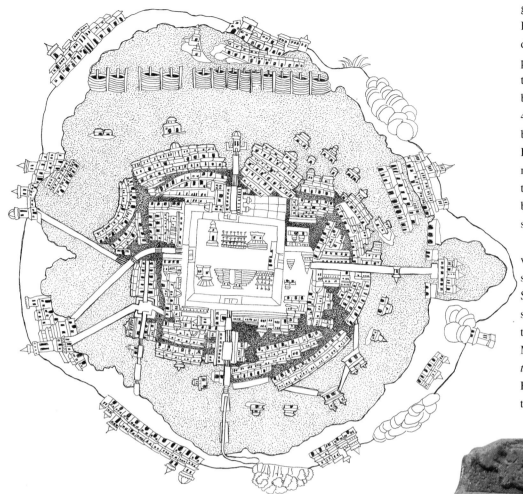

guise as Huitzilopochtli attests to his violent nature. His mother was the Earth Goddess, Coatlicue, who demanded human sacrifice to appease her for the pain she suffered in giving birth to the 400 Stars and to the Moon Goddess, Coyolxauhqui. When she became magically pregnant, her offspring, the 400 Night Gods, decided to kill her in punishment, but Coyolxauhqui ran to give her warning. Huitzilopochtli, springing forth fully armed as a warrior and hearing the sounds of a marching army, mistakenly cut off Coyolxauhqui's head and threw her body from the top of a mountain, before killing his siblings, the Night Gods.

Huitzilopochtli's birth, as one aspect of the Sun, was therefore a violent one, and each day at dawn he sallied forth to kill and destroy the Moon and Stars. So terrible was his vengeance that he demanded constant nourishment from the hearts and blood of captives to ensure he would emerge again from the Earth Mother each day. A grim testimony to this was the *tzompantli*, or skull rack, outside the Temple of Huitzilopochtli in Tlatelolco. Spanish reports tell us that this was a platform 180ft (54m) in length and

ABOVE
Plan of Tenochtitlan based on 16th-century Spanish observations. The city was planned with a ceremonial complex at its centre surrounded by residential and craftwork units.

RIGHT
Relief carving showing Tlaloc, the Rain God, as Lord of Tlalocan. Attached to his costume are the skulls of those who have died and entered his domain.

OPPOSITE
Aztec economy was supported by chinampas, *the so-called floating gardens. Those shown here at Xochimilco to the south of modern Mexico City are all that now remain of the* chinampa *system.*

Shown here is the Aztec temple of Santa Cecilia Acatitlan, which, although located near to Tenochtitlan, was never part of the Aztec capital city. It was used instead for ceremonies conducted by the local priesthood.

30ft (9m) wide on which were posts, each of which was strung with 20 skulls of sacrificed captives and placed so close together the skulls on one pole touched those on the next. Modern estimates suggest typical Spanish exaggeration in this account of the number of skulls. There were, nevertheless, *tzompantli* at several locations in Aztec cities, and each of these probably displayed in excess of 100 skulls.

Even the Aztec legends of the Toltecs, whom they regarded as a superior race from whom all goodness in the world flowed by the divine right of Quetzalcoatl, are tinged with the awesome powers of Tezcatlipoca/Huitzilopochtli. The legend tells us he appeared in the market-place as a naked Huastec merchant whose penis was so beautiful that the daughter of a noble of the city was overcome with desire. From their union came Huemac, the ill-fated ruler who oversaw the collapse of Toltec culture. Tezcatlipoca had a hand in this collapse too. He

LEFT
The planet Venus appeared both as Morning Star and Evening Star, which were held to have opposite qualities. Morning Star appeared as the precursor of the Sun, whereas Evening Star appeared after the Sun's descent into the Underworld. Xolotl, the Evening Star, is shown here as a distorted and horrifying figure.

OPPOSITE
ABOVE
This incense burner was used in the rituals dedicated to Tezcatlipoca, Smoking Mirror, and is made in the form of a turkey claw. The turkey was closely associated with Smoking Mirror. Aztec.

BELOW
Tezcatlipoca is identified here by his missing foot, which was lost when he engaged in combat with the Lords of the Underworld. He is shown dressed as a warrior and is eating the arm of a sacrificed captive. Aztec.

turned himself into a huge giant and allowed himself to be killed so that his rotting carcass would cause a plague in which thousands of Toltecs died. Even though the Aztec warrior-kings now claimed Toltec blood through their influential marriages, which meant their divine right to rule was sanctioned by Quetzalcoatl, it was nevertheless Tezcatlipoca who exercized power in the Aztec world.

Strangely enough, however, the Aztecs did not deify their rulers as warrior kings who impersonated this fearful God of War. Huitzilopochtli always remained a god of darkness who appeared only as a shadow spirit, who was never directly manifested in the human realm through impersonation, but who was capable of shape-changing and of inciting acts that, to us, are of particular barbarity. To the Aztec, such actions were justified by the fearful wrath of the

gods and the possible destruction of their world if blood offerings and sacrifices were not made in order to propitiate the gods and receive their blessing. The principle, in many ways, is not dissimilar from that of the Maya, who also felt that blood offerings were an essential part of their ritual life; although it is clear that the Aztec carried this to far greater extremes.

The extent of human sacrifice among the Aztecs has nevertheless undoubtedly been exaggerated. Although some sacrifices took place at regular intervals throughout the year, it is clear that most of these required only one victim amd that the maximum was originally four. It was only in the very late, and degenerate, period of Aztec history that large-scale slaughter of captives took place, and this occurred when the Aztec felt their own position to be insecure.

ABOVE
Lady Golden Bells, or Coyolxauhqui, was the most important aspect of the Moon. This aspect is symbolized in this stone carving by the moon-shaped nose pendant and the symbols on her ear ornaments indicating the lunar regulation of time.

OPPOSITE
Although identification is not certain, it is likely that this small obsidian mask represents Ixtilton, the lieutenant of Huitzilopochtli. Ixtilton visited children at night to bring them peaceful sleep.

It was more a means of reducing the effective fighting strength of their enemies than a requirement of ritual.

The ritual aspects of sacrifice seem to have had deep cultural roots for both the Aztec and their neighbours, as can be seen in the War of Flowers waged between the Aztec and their Tlaxcalan neighbours: theirs was an independent city-state which the Aztec never conquered. Despite its romantic title, the War of Flowers was actually a mock battle staged so that the élite warriors on each side could take the captives they required. The 'flowers' referred to were, in fact, the hearts of their victims, since blood spurting from a heart was shown in the murals as flowery spirals whirling from the opened chest cavity. Significantly, given that the Aztec royal lineage traced back to Tula, the War of Flowers appears to have originated among the Toltecs, since we find symbols at Tula referring to it. Thus the gods Quetzalcoatl and Tezcatlipoca must have been important to both the Toltecs and the Aztecs; it is simply that their dominance in maintaining social order was reversed. We should also bear in mind, since the élite warriors were pitched against each other, that the War of Flowers was also a testing ground for courage and that the capture of sacrificial victims was not its only objective.

While it is important to recognize the excesses of the Aztec wars and sacrifices, whereby the conquest of neighbouring groups enabled the Aztec to expand their empire to the point where it must have rivalled the former great empire of Teotihuacan, it is nevertheless a fact that the Aztec were, essentially, a farming people. Like the noble lineages, the warriors were an élite, known under the familiar names of Eagle and Jaguar warriors. There were other élite professions too, such as those of the merchant and the artisan; but a very large part of the Aztec population consisted of farmers who worked the *chinampas*, or raised fields, that spread throughout the Valley of Mexico. The huge increases in population that attended the establishment of the Aztec empire could never have been supported by tributes from subject towns, and the farmers were the mainstay of the Aztec economy.

Even though farmers themselves had little status, the importance of farming to the Aztec is reflected in the fact that all their festivals and ceremonies, including those of war, were organized around the agricultural year as recorded in the sacred calendrical texts. These were based on the calendar that had been in use by the Maya, and divided the year into 18 months of 20 days each with a five- day period at the

patron of the ninth month, was revered as the god who prevented disasters to the Aztec by ensuring success against their enemies, and that it was he who encouraged cruelty and deception but who also embodied the qualities of courage and nobility. In a similar way, although the Aztec said of Quetzalcoatl 'from him it began, from Quetzalcoatl it all flowed out, all art and knowledge', it must be considered due to Huitzilopochtli that Aztec life and the yearly round of activities, including those of agriculture, were maintained. In this sense we can see Huitzilopochtli as a god of the agricultural year just as surely as he was the god of warfare and darkness. The blood of the victims was seen as a form of nourishment, reflecting the old Maya idea that from death springs life.

A similar pre-occupation with the dual themes of death and life was evident at the annual agricultural festival of Tlacaxipeualiztla, which marked the first shoots of the young maize bursting forth from the seed. The deity celebrated here was Xipe Totec, patron of the second month and the god of springtime and the coming rains, but whose name translates as the Flayed Lord. He gains this name from his association with the maize bursting its skin, since at the height of the ritual a sacrificial captive was flayed alive and his skin donned either by the warrior who had captured him or the priest conducting the ceremony. The skin was sewn in place and worn until it rotted and the bindings burst open in a symbolic re-enactment of the bursting of the seed. But this also symbolized the necessity of death and burial – as the maize seed dies and is buried – so that renewal of life is possible.

The reliance on an essentially agricultural calendar to mark the onset of all ritual events resulted in a conservative approach to life in general. Nothing happened without the intercession of the gods, and since the gods were firmly rooted in the seasonal pattern little variation could be permitted for individual innovation. Because of this the Aztec had a strong belief in fate; a sense that one was born with one's future already mapped out. The complex pantheon of deities, most of them with varying and often opposing attributes, also fuelled this sense of fatalism. Only the priests, trained in the secrets of the calendars and their interpretation, had access to the knowledge of the gods, and this was complicated by the fact that the Aztec, in addition to the agricultural calendar of 365 days, used a second parallel ritual calendar of 260 days to compute significant events. It was therefore only they who were able to conduct the major ceremonies with the exactitude and preci-

end of the year that was unnamed. This five-day period, known as Nemontemi, the barren days, was considered to bring portents of evil, and during this period all the people stayed quietly indoors, utensils were smashed, and the fires extinguished, while the occupants of the buildings offered silent prayers that the period would end without disaster. The other months, however, were each under the patronage of a different deity and offerings were made to the appropriate deity at the beginning of each month.

We have already seen that Huitzilopochtli,

ABOVE
A reconstructed drawing of a stone altar depicting the Moon Goddess. In a dispute with the other sky deities, she was killed and her body dismembered. She is shown here with severed head, arms and legs.

OPPOSITE
The Flayed Lord, Xipe Totec, symbolically represented the sprouting of maize, and was therefore associated with cults of fertility and growth.

sion they required. For most people the gods and priests simply had an unquestioned presence and personal sacrifices, both great and small, were an inevitable part of life.

Everything in the Aztec world tended to confirm this view. Even the pyramid built in the middle of Tenochtitlan and dedicated to the dual deities Tlaloc (the Rain God) and Huizilopochtli was a constant reminder of Serpent Mountain; the centre of the Aztec cosmos. Over the years, as new pyramids were built to encase the old ones and their rich caches of offerings of precious goods, the sacred

power imbedded in such a building increased. As the most important Aztec town, Tenochtitlan was the centre of their empire and the pyramid – or Serpent Mountain – was the centre of their world both at a spiritual and a temporal level. At its heart, Tenochtitlan therefore bore a symbol of authority over all aspects of the Aztec realm. Furthermore, Serpent Mountain acted as both the entrance to the Underworld and as access to the celestial realms. The fates of the people were as surely bound up in this interaction as was the fate of a sacrificial victim who gave blood to sustain life.

LEFT
During the agricultural festival of Tlacaxipeualiztli, the priests of Xipe Totec donned the flayed skin of a sacrificial victim, which was worn until the skin rotted and fell away. The ceremony symbolized the bursting of the skin of the maize seed. Xipe Totec is shown here dressed in flayed skin which has been sewn into place. Aztec.

OPPOSITE
Shown here is the back of a carving of the head of Xipe Totec, on which is a symbol associating him with Tezatlipoca, Smoking Mirror. Xipe Totec was an aspect of Smoking Mirror who was closely associated with suffering and sacrifice. Aztec.

Following this principle, other temples of the city were intended as representations of symbolic landscapes, or architectural features were erected in natural settings to enhance and give access for people to the sacred powers that already existed there. Thus Nezahualcoyotl, or Fasting Coyote, the ruler of Texcoco, remodelled the Sacred Hill of Tezcotzingo in the form of a cosmological diagram dedicated to Chalchiuhtlicue, the Water Goddess and sister of the Rain Gods, or Tlalocs. Tezcotzingo, with its aqueducts and basins, therefore became a symbol for the power of Chalchiuhtlicue as well as the region from which her power was manifested. Significantly the region of Tezcotzingo was itself supplied with water from Mount Tlaloc, the abode of the Chalchiuhtlicue's brothers the Rain Gods.

Every element in the Aztec world was, therefore, a constant reminder of the role the deities had to play in maintaining order and of the indivisible links between the celestial, middle, and lower realms. These were never considered as disjointed or separated spheres, but as a continuum. All these principles were also evident at an even more personal level, since the human body itself was conceived as a representation of the cosmos, with the head, heart, and liver corresponding to the three divisions. Of these the heart was animated by a force called *teyolia*, or divine fire, a presence that also existed in sacred mountains, temples, and so forth. Human sacrifice is perhaps more readily understood in this context: just as the sacred fires burning in temples or the rituals dedicated to the gods 'gave life' and animated the world, so the human heart 'gave life' to the body. Through sacrifice and the offering of a heart, life was in effect being given back to the gods.

In spite of the harsh realities of the ritual performances, there is another side to Aztec life which is frequently overlooked. This was their basic humility. The Spanish reports of Aztec deities and the ceremonies related to them often leave out important

important was this that there was a special class of nobles known as *tlamatinime* who were trained to use language in an attempt to find out the ultimate truth and its relationship to human nature. Among their tasks was the posing of riddles which asked fundamental questions, the construction of metaphors and proverbs, the organization of rhetorical speeches, and the composition of poetry.

It is significant that when a poet composed a particularly fine verse, or indeed when a muralist managed to convey an accurate impression, he became filled with the same *teyolia*, or divine fire, that was released when the heart of a captive was given as an offering. Here too we find yet another juxtaposition of ideas which express the dualities present in every facet of life. It is of further interest to note the connection with the Aztec War of Flowers, which secured the *teyolia* of hearts to give life to the gods, and the phrase 'flower and song' to mean poetry and truth by which the poet became filled with *teyolia* power. Closely linked with the concept of poetry and language is the use of dance and song, which were sometimes so closely linked that the poems were actually sung to the rhythm of a drum. Every great lord had his own poets, composers, and dancers to write and perform new compositions on the occasion of public feasts and ceremonies.

The sentiments being expressed above are a far

As part of their divinatory role, Aztec priests attempted to obtain visions of future events. To achieve this, they would gaze into highly polished obsidian mirrors in which they would see clouds of smoke that cleared to reveal a prophesy.

details of sacrifice, not because the Aztec were ashamed to admit them but because they did not want to risk hurting the feelings of the friars who were recording their traditions. This 'gentle' side of Aztec life is evident in the education they gave their children, since they were taught in schools that emphasized the essential qualities of obedience, diligence, humility, self-discipline, and rhetoric. The children of the more élite families were, in addition, taught history, arithmetic, agriculture, astronomy, architecture, and, of course, warfare. The inclusion of rhetoric serves to introduce important aspects of life: the emphasis placed on public speaking and the Aztec love of poetry. Even the warrior-kings were known by a name which translates as Great Speaker.

This emphasis on the spoken word is in some ways the duality that balances the sacrificial aspects of ritual. Just as things could be brought into being by the violent act of sacrifice, so could they be motivated and understood through the spoken word. So

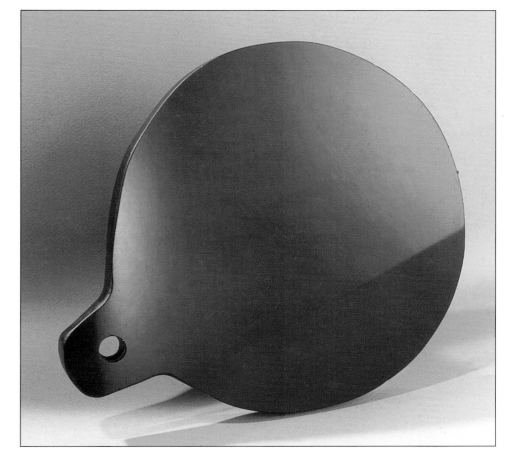

remove from the more usual picture that is painted of the Aztecs as savage barbarians whose entire lives centred on warfare, conquest, and sacrifice. It is also very different from the image of unsophisticated Chichimeca hunter-warriors acting as mercenary troops for the more highly developed remnants of the former Toltec state. In less than 200 years the Chichimeca had evolved into an Aztec empire which, although suffused with acts of undeniable violence, was nevertheless capable of expressing sentiments of the utmost subtlety and beauty. It is difficult to reconcile these two opposites unless we view them from the Aztec perspective. Everything was dual and had its opposing force contained within itself, and this applied to the totality of the culture as well as to the minutiae of individual expressions. To the Aztec gentleness had to come out of violence, in exactly the same way as life came from death.

Both of course were expressions of the gods as well as of the people, since the duality extends here: the individual is also a microcosm, containing within himself all the forces of the world in their purest form.

But something happened to disturb this world. Despotic leaders, eager to enhance their own power or in deliberate acts of genocide against their neighbours, permitted the Aztec balance between humility and hostility to lose its equilibrium. Huitzilopochtli, in his role of unrelenting cruelty, was allowed to grow in strength, until, shortly before the Spanish arrived in the early 1500s, Aztec armies of 16,000 or more Eagle and Jaguar warriors were marching against rivals who could not offer resistance. They brought in thousands of victims for the sacrificial altars and for the dedication of Tenochtitlan's new temples. By 1508 the Aztec ruler Moctezuma had achieved his aim: all of Anahuac (ancient Mexico) was under his control, and this control was absolute. Moctezuma ruled not by decree, but by divine right.

Yet something in this imbalance must have disturbed Moctezuma. As Great Speaker of the Aztecs his patron deity was the mighty and deadly Huitzilopochtli. It was Huitzilopochtli who had brought Anahuac to heel and had crushed any active resistance. It was he who had been responsible for the slaughter of the thousands of warriors whose hearts had been offered up to him. Yet Moctezuma held his position through a Toltec lineage dedicated to Quetzalcoatl, Huitzilopochtli's twin rival, and he had also been born in a year dedicated to the Feathered Serpent. Moctezuma knew, perhaps better than anyone else, that a confrontation between Quetzalcoatl and Huitzilopochtli was imminent. Moctezuma was also a priest, and understood from reading the calendars that they were close to the year Ce Acatl (One Reed), the end of a 52-year calendrical cycle when the world would either be renewed or destroyed.

Ce Acatl would occur once in Moctezuma's lifetime, beginning in the spring of 1519. Hernando Cortés arrived in Tenochtitlan in November 1519, coincidently during the month dedicated to Huitzilopochtli, and there can be little doubt that, initially at least, Moctezuma must have seen this as the returning Coatzacoatl come to make the final challenge to his rival. The inevitable happened. Moctezuma was killed, and although the Aztec warriors continued to put up a spirited resistance against the Spanish and their Indian allies, by 1521 the siege of Tenochtitlan was over. The victorious Spanish

then systematically destroyed the pyramids, temples, and palaces and and declared the Aztec site the capital of New Spain. In just two years the Spanish successfully obliterated 3,000 years of Mesoamerican civilization.

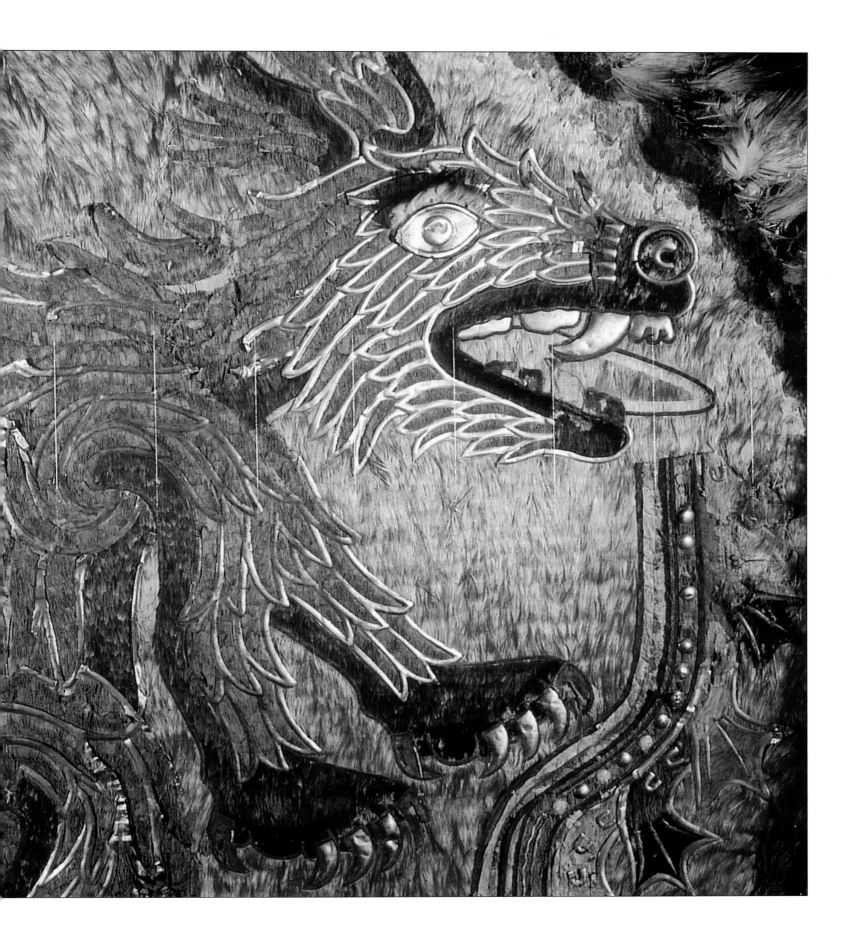

INDEX

INDEX

INDEX

INDEX

Shown here are reconstructed and restored temples and temple platforms from the Toltec-Maya side of Chichén Itzá in the Yucatán peninsula.

ACKNOWLEDGEMENTS

The Publishers would like to thank the following suppliers of illustrations:

Norman Bancroft Hunt 23, drawing 46-47, drawing 53 top, 68 top, 72 top, 72 bottom, drawing 76 right, drawing 86 top, drawing 96. Museum für Völkerkunde, Berlin, Germany 66. Nick Saunders 4, 29, 35, 54 top.

The following photographs have been supplied by Werner Forman Archive:

Anthropology Museum, Veracruz University, Jalapa 20 both, 31, jacket back cover. David Bernstein, New York 12. Biblioteca Universitaria, Bologna, Italy 36-37, 54 bottom. British Museum, London 9, 10-11, 30, 34, 44, 83, 90 top, 101, 103, front cover centre inset. Dallas Museum of Art, U.S.A. 21, 32, 61, 74-75, 76 left. Philip Goldman, London 47. Liverpool Museum, Liverpool, England 90 bottom. Merrin Collection 41. Metropolitan Museum of Art, New York, U.S.A, lent by the Republic of Guatemala 73. National Museum of Anthropology, Mexico City 13, 14, 16-17, 21, 24, 26-27, 42-43, 48-49, 53 bottom, 56-57, 62, 63, 64-65, 68 bottom, 70, 71, 77, 78-79, 86, 87, 88-89, 93, 94, 104-105, 110-111, front cover bottom inset. Museum für Völkerkunde, Basel, Switzerland 2, 55, 92, 99, 102. Museum für Völkerkunde, Berlin, Germany 22, 80, 91. Museum fur Völkerkunde, Hamburg, Germany 3, 97, 98. National Museum of Natural History, Smithsonian Institute, Washington, U.S.A. 100. Pigorini Museum of Prehistory and Ethnology, Rome 4, front cover main picture. Private Collections 18, 52, 69, front cover top inset. By courtesy of Sotheby's, New York 59. St. Louis Art Museum, U.S.A. 95.